Wellbeing for kids

Making kids smarter, happier

STAGES 7-9

Kate Daniels & Victoria Pugh

HC CB
HARPERCOLLINS CHILDREN'S BOOKS

First published by Collins
This edition published in India in 2024 by HarperCollins *Children's Books*
An imprint of HarperCollins *Publishers* India
Building No 10, Tower A, 4th Floor, DLF Cyber City, Phase II,
Gurugram – 122002

2 4 6 8 10 9 7 5 3 1

P-ISBN: 978-93-6569-987-6

William Collins' dream of knowledge for all began with the publication of his first book in 1819.
A self-educated mill worker, he not only enriched millions of lives, but also founded a flourishing publishing house. Today, staying true to this spirit, Collins books are packed with inspiration, innovation and practical expertise.
They place you at the centre of a world of possibility and give you exactly what you need to explore it.
Collins. Freedom to teach.

Series editor: Kate Daniels
Author: Victoria Pugh
Publisher: Elaine Higgleton
Author of the introduction: Becky Goddard-Hill
Product developer: Roisin Leahy
Development and copy editor: Jo Kemp
Proofreader: Claire Throp

Illustrations by Jouve India Ltd.
Cover design by Shamika Chaves

Typeset by Sam Vail, Ken Vail Graphic Design

Printed and bound at Nutech Print Services - India

HarperCollinsIn

Contents

Contents

Stage 8

Contents

Stage 9

LETTER TO PARENTS/GUARDIAN

Dear parent or guardian,

Welcome to the Collins International Wellbeing course, and the start of your child's wellbeing journey.

Collins supports this learning journey for your child through the materials in this course, and we'd like you, as parents/guardians, to be part of the experience. This letter explains how the course works, and how you can help your child to get the maximum benefit from the Collins materials.

What is the Collins Wellbeing course?

Concerns around the wellbeing of children have grown since the Covid-19 pandemic; children might have spent more time at home during the pandemic than they otherwise would have, and this has had an impact on the development of children's language and social skills, and sense of self. The Collins Wellbeing materials have been written to support parents/guardians who need to help their children navigate a world that may be unfamiliar to them, and to help support young children who need help developing their social skills, and who may be more anxious about social interactions than children used to be.

Children learn most in the first five years of life: the early years and time spent in kindergarten and nursery are recognised as the essential foundations for success at school. Millions of children will have missed out on essential formative experiences in nurseries and kindergartens because of the pandemic, and schools are now having to help children catch up. Gaps in learning – caused in this instance by the pandemic – are being recognised widely; there are similar gaps in the emotional and personal development of young children. The Collins Wellbeing course has been designed to help ensure that children are fully supported in terms of their social, personal and emotional development.

Similarly, the secondary course has been designed to support older children who have had big gaps in their social experiences of school and relationships with peers, due to the pandemic, at a formative time in their development. Our research with teachers has particularly highlighted increased anxiety in older students, especially around things like giving presentations in school, and how they manage their feelings of anxiety in different settings, and the course has been designed specifically to support that.

There is a large body of research that highlights the important benefits for children's future and achievements of focusing on wellbeing. Research suggests strong links between student wellbeing and improved academic achievement (Kirkcaldy et al., 2004; Suldo et al., 2011), while incidents of academic underachievement are associated with poorer student wellbeing (van Batenburg-Eddes & Jolles, 2013).

Other characteristics such as self-confidence and growth mindset, both of which are important for academic success, have been linked with higher student wellbeing (King, 2017), and students with lower wellbeing have been found to be at a greater risk of behavioural difficulties and school drop-out compared to their peers with higher levels of wellbeing (Arslan & Renshaw, 2018).

As such, we hope you'll agree that it is essential to support your child's wellbeing effectively.

The Covid pandemic is just one example of an event that has caused gaps in learning; this course aims to provide your children with the tools and resilience required to cope well in a range of scenarios.

Being involved as a parent/guardian

There is nothing covered in this course that should raise concerns for you. Topics covered include: identifying and managing emotions; developing healthy habits; establishing healthy relationships with peers, and how to cope when these change; being a part of a community; how to stay safe in school, at home and online; how to cope with change; and how to live sustainably and ethically.

The book that your child will be using is a workbook that they can write into, and can be used as a record of the topics they have covered, as well as something that they can refer back to in order to recap things they have learned to support their wellbeing.

Using this resource

While most of the lessons in the book will require some amount of engagement and intervention from you as the parent/guardian and will be self explanatory, there are a few chapters that will require you to be more hands-on and organize activities to drive the lesson home. Please scan this QR code to access the Wellbeing Parents' Guide, which will have detailed activities as well as lesson plans for your child.

We hope you make the most of this resource and encourage the wellbeing of your child.

Harper Collins Team

Wellbeing for kids

Making kids smarter, happier

STAGE 7

Hello and welcome to Wellbeing Stage 7!

Changes

Stage 7 brings with it a lot of change; perhaps you have moved school or at least moved into a new class and a new stage in your education.

Working through these wellbeing activities will help you to understand and cope better with the changes that are happening to you, not only at school but also in your brain and in your body as you go through puberty. They should help to make things less confusing.

Mixed feelings

New experiences and change can be exciting but scary too and that's okay. Feelings are complicated and we can have lots of different emotions all at the same time. By learning to recognise and identify your feelings and ways to express and manage them you will feel more in control of them.

Taking care of yourself

As you work through this workbook you will also learn some brilliant ways to take care of yourself. Self-kindness makes everything easier and learning how to look after your body and your mind is really useful.

There are some simple things like getting enough good sleep and spending time in nature that will help make you feel better and knowing what works for you is powerful!

Relationships

Friendships matter and knowing how to be a good friend is also something we are going to look at as well as ways to handle bullying. It is important to keep safe – both in real life and online – so we are going to look at that too.

Are you ready to learn some fantastic ways to help you feel stronger and more confident?

Let's make a start.

May your year ahead be as BRILLIANT as you are!

Becky Goddard-Hill

Unit 7.1 Feelings and emotions

What do you know?

- What do you know about emotions?
- What do you think the photograph shows?
- How openly do you express your emotions? Why do you think this?

In this unit, you will:

- Understand how different situations can cause a lot of mixed feelings.
- Learn how puberty affects our emotions and feelings.
- Consider how change and loss can be experienced by different people.

Lesson 1 Our complex emotions

Activity 1.1a Emotions challenge

How many emotions do you know of? Time yourself and see how many you can answer. If you're feeling competitive, sit with a friend and try writing down as many of them as you can in five minutes. Your challenge is to see how many emotions you can write down in the time.

A ______________ N ______________

B ______________ O ______________

C ______________ P ______________

D ______________ Q ______________

E ______________ R ______________

F ______________ S ______________

G ______________ T ______________

H ______________ U ______________

I ______________ V ______________

J ______________ W ______________

K ______________ X ______________

L ______________ Y ______________

M ______________ Z ______________

Lesson 1 Our complex emotions

Activity 1.1b How do they feel?

Our feelings can be quite complex. In different situations we may have a real mix of emotions. Use the examples below to consider which feelings someone might feel in each situation and why. The first one has been done for you.

Statement	Which feelings?	Why might they feel this way?
I am about to go on stage. This is a dream come true! I'm so sweaty and my throat feels weird. I really hope I remember my lines.	Excited, happy, alive, nervous, anxious, scared	They are doing something they love and have wanted to do for a long time, so they feel really good, but they are also nervous that they might mess it up.
I love my mum but she just got really angry with me in front of my friends. I get why – I was being really rude to her – but now she's gone out, all my friends are laughing at me.		
My best friend has been so excited about us going to see a film premiere together and it's tonight. I promised I would go ages ago but I've had such a busy day I'd really rather stay in. But I don't want to let my friend down.		
My dad has just been offered this amazing job. It would be so much more money for our family and we'd live in this really cool new city, but I have all my friends here and I love where we live now.		

Can you think of any situations where you have had a mix of emotions? Write the situation below, adding all of the different emotions you felt, as you did in the table on the previous page.

Lesson 2 Our adolescent brains

Activity 1.2a Puberty and me

Currently, you are in your adolescent phase, which refers to the stage of transitioning from a child to an adult. This stage has several mental and physical changes, which collectively are termed as puberty. It is important to remember that the pace of transition is not the same for everyone, and that is fine. But it is important to understand these changes when they do happen.

Using the space below, write or draw all of the emotional changes or behaviour you have noticed in yourself recently/in the last few months/years.

Puberty and me

Lesson 2 Our adolescent brains

Activity 1.2b The effects of puberty on your changing emotions

Research the science behind what is happening in the brain during puberty. Create a 'What I know' mind map to show what you know about the changes in the brain and our emotions during puberty.

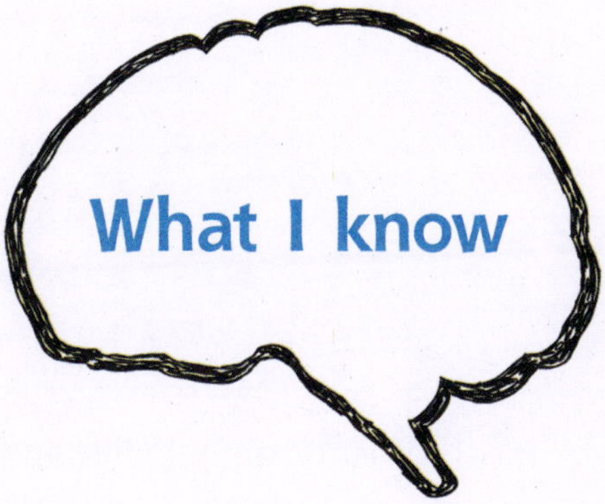

Lesson 3 Grief

Activity 1.3a The grief cycle

While loss and grief cause sadness, they are a part of our lives, and we need to understand how they function if we have to accept it and move forward. Grief can be different for everyone and people can react in very different ways. There is no right or wrong way to deal with grief as long as you are dealing with it. There are, however, recognised stages that someone is likely to go through during a big loss or change. Talk to an adult about it before looking up the varied stages and their definitions online.

The following stages have been jumbled up. Can you put them in the order in which people most commonly go through them, and write down your understanding of how each stage might feel, using what you have just learned?

BARGAINING – ACCEPTANCE – DENIAL – DEPRESSION – ANGER

Stage	How might someone feel or act during this stage?
1. 2. 3. 4. 5.	

Which do you feel would be the most difficult to deal with and why? Give reasons for your views.

Unit reflection

In this unit you have been thinking about identifying emotions.

You have learned about our complex emotions, how puberty affects our emotions and how it is possible to grieve healthily.

Write the biggest thing you have learned in the sun, write other things you have learned in the clouds around it, and write things you want to learn more about on the petals of the flower.

Unit 7.2 Navigating our emotions

What do you know?

- How has this tree been able to survive?
- How can we relate this to our human experiences?

In this unit, you will:

- Understand what resilience looks like.
- Consider wellbeing in the context of self-image.
- Learn about self-care and being kind to ourselves and others.

Lesson 1 Resilience

Activity 2.1a The girl who fell from the sky

Read the extract below, then talk to your parent/guardian about what you would do if this had happened to you.

Despite the trauma of this experience, she realised at once what had happened. Looking up at the trees she knew she had survived an air disaster, probably because her seat had broken the fall as she crashed through the dense foliage.

Unsurprisingly, the seventeen-year-old was in considerable pain and feeling dizzy. She had broken her collarbone, damaged a ligament in one knee, and sustained deep cuts and bruises as she hit the ground. Her left eye was also swollen shut, but she could still walk and knew she had to start finding a way to safety.

Koepcke had learned enough about the jungle from her parents to know it wasn't as dangerous as people liked to think. Travelling on foot, it was important to keep a cool head and not do anything foolish, but she had no idea where she was, or where any of the other passengers had come down. She had also lost a shoe and her glasses, which complicated things as she was very short-sighted. Nor was she dressed for a jungle trek, with only a light cotton summer dress to protect her from the hordes of biting, stinging insect that were buzzing all around her.

While you listen to the rest of the story, note down anything you hear that you think is a sign of Juliane's resilience.

Lesson 1 Resilience

Activity 2.1b Short story plan

Write your own story of resilience. Use this page to plan your short story. You can either rewrite Juliane's story, imagining what you would do in her situation and how you would use resilience to survive. Or write another story imagining yourself in a different situation where you have to be resilient to succeed.

Who is/are the main character/characters? ______________________________

____

____

Where are they? ____

____

____

What is the problem? ____

____

How will the story start? _______________________________________

____

____

What action will happen in the middle? ___________________________

____

____

How will the character/characters show resilience? _________________

____

____

How will the story end? ____

____

____

Lesson 2 Wellbeing

Activity 2.2a Are you kind to yourself, or are you your own worst enemy?

Reflect on this below, considering these questions: What are you like when you are alone? Do you speak kindly to yourself or are you mean to yourself? Do you have an inner critic? How loud is it? Is the person you portray and the way you act true to yourself, or are you just copying others and trying to fit in?

Lesson 2 Wellbeing

Activity 2.2b Reflection

While it is good to know what others think of you, what we think of ourselves and how we are is just as important, if not more. It allows us to interact with other people in a productive way, and also makes us mindful of our actions outside.

Grab a partner, it can be a friend, a sibling, or a classmate you know well, and write a short note on how you see them and what you think of them, and have them do the same. After you both are done, exchange your notes to see whether your self-image is the same as the image others have of you. And remember to be kind. Using what your partner has written, answer the questions below independently, spending some time to reflect quietly on this experience and what you can take from it.

What did your partner say about you? ____________________

____

____

____

Were you surprised about what your partner saw in you? Why? ____________________

____

____

____

Has it made you question anything you thought about yourself? Explain. ____________________

____

____

____

How can you build on this experience to re-evaluate your self-image and self-awareness? ____________________

____

____

____

Is there anything else you want to note or to explore further regarding your wellbeing or self-image? ____________________

____

____

____

Lesson 3 Self-care

Activity 2.3 Habits and activities

What sorts of habits or activities can you think of that would be self-caring?
Write or draw and label them below.

Unit reflection

You have just completed a unit on managing emotions. You have learned about resilience, the impact our words and actions can have on our own and others' wellbeing, and how to bring self-care strategies into our lives.

1. How can these lessons help you to manage your emotions now and in the future?

2. What new things are you going to try or to bring into your life?

3. Who can help you with these?

4. What more would you like to know or have help with?

Unit 7.3 Body health

What do you know?

- Why might this picture portray someone who is healthy?
- What do you do that is healthy?

In this unit, you will:

- Learn about the problems associated with inactivity.
- Understand why rest and sleep are so important.
- Recognise why spending time outside and in nature is so beneficial.

Lesson 1 Inactive to active

Activity 3.1a How does exercise improve our health?

Write down as many ideas as you can think of below and discuss them with an adult. Remember that health is not just physical health, but mental and emotional health too.

Lesson 1 Inactive to active

Activity 3.1b Health coach

Imagine that you are an online health coach. Inactive people are messaging about problems they have, all of which are linked directly to their sedentary (inactive) lifestyles. These people want to be fit but they keep being lazy, watching TV or going on their phones/games console. Create three patients/problems and then think of active solutions for them all. Ask the adults in your family for their suggestions too.

Describe the problem/health issue.

Person 1: ______________________________

____

____

Person 2: ______________________________

____

____

Person 3: ______________________________

____

____

Describe what you have advised.

Person 1: ______________________________

____

____

Person 2: ______________________________

____

____

Person 3: ______________________________

____

____

Lesson 2 Sleep

Activity 3.2a Sleep quiz

Sleeping is one of the most important parts of our lives. Did you know that people on average spend close to 26 years of their lives sleeping? Talk to your parent/guardian about the importance of sleep, and look up online to find out what happens to the body and mind when we sleep. After that, answer the questions below.

1. How many hours of sleep do you think 11–12-year-olds need each night?

____

2. How does a lack of sleep affect you physically?

____

____

____

____

3. How does a lack of sleep affect you mentally and emotionally?

____

____

____

____

4. How many hours a night do you think you sleep?

____

5. If you find it hard to sleep, what helps you?

____

____

____

____

Lesson 2 Sleep

Activity 3.2b Before and after

It's time to create a comic strip for sleep! On the top two panels, draw what happens to a person who does not get enough sleep. Use the left panel to draw their state before going off to sleep, and on the right, show them after they haven't had a good night's rest. On the bottom panel, show the before and after for a person who has healthy sleeping habits.

Lesson 3 Nature

Activity 3.3a My sketch and notes of my natural place

It's time to fire up your imagination! Sit upright but comfortably and close your eyes. In your imagination you are going to go to a natural place that you know and love. Take three deep breaths in and out to relax yourself. Picture the natural place in your mind and look around to see it better. Think slowly about what you see and feel – any colours, views, sensations, the temperature, smells. When you're ready, slowly open your eyes and have a stretch. Then, with this image still fresh in your mind, sketch it below. Feel free to add any features you think would look good.

Lesson 3 Nature

Activity 3.3b Reflection

What healthy habits do you already have? What new healthy habits do you want to try next? Use this page to write down your thoughts and what you have learned in this unit.

Unit reflection

Look back through this unit in your workbook and reflect on all that you have learned. Remember that you will always have your natural place that you sketched in your imagination, and you can return to it anytime you feel big emotions. Pull out two key things you learned from each lesson and jot them down in the diamonds below.

Unit 7.4 Different friendships

What do you know?

- This topic is all about friends and healthy relationships. Before we start, what do you already know about friendships?
- Set your mind free and doodle it all down in the space below. It can go from good to bad and everything in between.
- Any burning questions about friendships? You can use this space to ask your parent/guardian too.

In this unit, you will:

- Explore what makes a friend a friend.
- Consider what a healthy relationship is.
- Learn how to end friendships positively.

Lesson 1 Friendships

Activity 4.1a Types of friendship

Think about yourself and the people around you. What do you feel or observe about different types of friendships? Can you define what the differences are between different types of friends?

A good friend is ____

A best friend is ____

A friend of a friend is ____

Lesson 1 Friendships

Activity 4.1b Meeting new people

Some people may make it look easy to make friends or talk to new people. However, they may be just as nervous as you inside. It's important to remember that everyone can feel nervous from time to time. So, if you're in a new situation, such as a new school, a new class, a new sporting activity or a social event where you don't know anybody, here's a list to help you.

Top tips on how to make meeting new people easier

1. Use calm breathing to help you feel positive about meeting new people.
2. Scan the room to see who you might like to talk to.
3. Notice how other people are in the room. There may be people standing alone who have nobody to talk to and would welcome you talking to them.
4. Listen to what groups of people are talking about and join in the conversation if the topic is interesting.
5. Trust your gut feelings. You'll probably know within the first minute whether you want to talk more with somebody, or if you need to politely move on and talk to somebody else.
6. Approach somebody and either ask their name or start a conversation about what other people are talking about.
7. Remember to make eye contact and smile when you introduce yourself to another person, if you feel comfortable doing this.
8. Listen to what the other person is saying.
9. People like shared experiences where they connect with other people. So, if a person plays the same video game, likes the same music, supports the same sports team or lives in the same area as you, comment on this and make that connection.
10. Be fine with rejection. If you talk to five people and you don't have anything in common with four of them, or they don't want to talk to you, that is fine, because the fifth person may turn out to be a really good friend – and that's all that matters.

Study the advice given in the tips on the previous page.

List the three pieces of advice that you think are most useful and say why. Then share them with some of your friends and family members, and get them to share their tips too.

Advice	Why is it useful?

Lesson 2 Healthy friendships

Activity 4.2 What makes a healthy friendship?

With an adult and a friend, discuss the meaning of a healthy relationship. After your discussion, write down in the figures below what makes a healthy friendship, and who is a genuine friend.

Lesson 3 Friends forever?

Activity 4.3a Best friends forever?

What do you think about this statement?

Is it always true? Do best friends always remain best friends? Discuss this separately with a friend and adult family members.

Why do you think this?

Lesson 3 Friends forever?

Activity 4.3b Best friends forever?

We used to be such good friends. We met on our first day of school. He made me laugh when I felt sad about leaving my mum. He was always good at making me laugh.

When we heard that we were going to different schools we were both so sad. On our last day of primary school we signed each other's shirts 'Best friends forever'. We hung out all summer playing football and messing around in the park.

On our first day of our new schools we called each other that night and talked about how it went, and then we hung out as usual at the weekend. We kept doing that for the first few weeks and then one day he didn't turn up when he said he would.

I messaged him: 'Where are you?'

'Oh, sorry. A couple of school friends invited me over and I lost track of time. Next weekend?'

On Friday the next weekend he messaged to say he couldn't make it again.

'Can I come and join you? Be good to meet your friends...' I messaged.

No reply.

It was weird, like suddenly something had changed; he had changed.

Walking back from school the next week I caught sight of him ahead. I ran to catch him up. I was so pleased to see him.

'All right,' he said, all cool and weird – his voice sounded all different. He didn't even act like he knew me, let alone like he was my best friend!

As I stood there shocked, he just walked away, said something to his friends and laughed. That really hurt.

What do you think has happened in the story above? What do you think the boy in the story should do? And what would be the positive thing to do here? After reflecting on these questions, finish the story. What happens next?

Unit reflection

Reread the poem by John Foster below. Can you add some extra lines on using what you have learned in this unit?

A friend is...

A friend is someone you can rely on
A shoulder to cry on.
A friend is someone who cares.
A friend is someone who shares.
A friend is someone who won't let you down
Someone who sticks by your side.
A friend is someone who listens to you
And in whom you can confide.
A friend is someone who won't force you
To do things you don't want to do.
A friend is someone who will always
Keep their promises to you.
A friend is someone you can trust.
A friend is loyal and true
Someone you can depend on
Who is always there for you.

John Foster

Unit 7.5 Standing up for ourselves

What do you know?

- How can you be good to yourself and others day to day?

In this unit, you will:

- Learn how to find positive solutions in times of conflict.
- Learn the value of being your true self.
- Explore bullying behaviour and its impacts.

Lesson 1 Resolving conflict

Activity 5.1a Conflict scenarios

You're trying to get ready for school. Your brother is in the bathroom again and is taking so long. He does this every morning and it frustrates you and makes you late! You shout at him and he shouts back...

A new student came to join your class a few weeks ago and the teacher asked your best friend to look after them. The new student still won't leave you both alone and it's really getting on your nerves. You start ignoring them and giving them dirty looks when your friend isn't looking, but they both see you and your friend shouts at you. You feel ready to explode...

Using one of the examples above, answer the questions below.

1. What do you think of this reaction? Why do you think this?

2. Where do you think these reactions and actions will lead? Explain some outcomes which could occur.

3. How could this situation have been avoided? Give some examples.

4. What could you do to resolve this positively? Try to add details and examples.

Lesson 1 Resolving conflict

Activity 5.1b My little page of calm

This is a page where you can add your thoughts, tips and exercises for keeping calm.

Lesson 2 This is me!

Activity 5.2a Reflection

With your parent/guardian, watch the music video of 'This is Me!' Now that you have seen it, try expressing yourself or who you are through dance or a song. What step or verse would define you? Describe what you did and how it felt doing the activity in this lesson.

How does it feel when you are truly yourself without worrying who other people are? You can write or draw a self-portrait to describe/show this!

If anything about being you makes you feel worried, make sure you talk to an adult you trust.

Lesson 2 This is me!

Activity 5.2b All about me

This page is a bonus page – all about you! You can add doodles or words or stick in pictures all about you.

Lesson 3 Bullying

Activity 5.3 Thoughts or poems

With your parent/guardian, discuss bullying, and how it differs from banter or joking. Then, thinking about the poems you read, try writing your own poem about bullying.

Who can you go to see in school if you are worried about anything to do with bullying? Write a list of who these people are here so that you can remember and also tell your friends.

Unit reflection

How would you rate your new skills at conflict resolution out of 10 and why?

How would you rate your ability to be authentically yourself out of 10 and why?

1 2 3 4 5 6 7 8 9 10

What have the poems encouraged you to think about regarding bullying?

Is there anything you want to learn more about or are worried about?

Unit 7.6 Safe aware

What do you know?

- About keeping yourself safe?

In this unit, you will answer these questions:

- Are online friends, friends?
- Do you know how to stay safe everywhere?
- How would you deal with an emergency?

Lesson 1 Social media

Activity 6.1a What's happening here?

What's happening in this photograph? Note down your suggestions to create a mind map with the photo at the centre.

Lesson 1 Social media

Activity 6.1b Getting ready for social media

Getting ready for social media by Internet Matters.

1. Research. Is this app OK for my age? Is it safe? (Your parent or carer can read some reviews with you to help you decide. Avoid apps where people are anonymous because this makes them feel they can say or do anything hurtful to others.)
2. Check the age restrictions – most apps require you to be at least 13 or older to use – be honest about your age – this is so you do not lose out on any protection the app or site has built-in.
3. Email – if you are asked to give an email address, use a family email address. Not one that is yours alone.
4. Create a secure password – don't use words or names that are easy to guess, like names of your pets or your favourite band. Try mixing random words up, using upper and lower case, numbers and special characters and never share your password with anyone except your parents or carers.
5. Avoid using your full name or anyone else's.
6. Set up your privacy settings – get an adult to help you to make it 'private' (not 'public').
7. Do not share any personal information about yourself or others and only share posts or stories with close friends and family.
8. Profile picture or other photos – make sure your photo does not show where you live or go to school in the background of your photo. Avoid having photos that show street corners where someone can see the street name.
9. Family agreement – your family may have agreed on some rules about what is OK to share or read online – stick to these as they are there to keep you safe.

Which three points do you think are the most important? Why?

How will doing these nine things keep you safe if you decide to go on to a social media app or website?

Lesson 2 Keeping safe out and about

Activity 6.2a What do you like to do?

Where do you like to go and what do you like to do when you're not at school or at home? Feel free to draw, write, or even paste pictures.

Lesson 2 Keeping safe out and about

Activity 6.2b Reflection

How would you keep safe when you're at your favourite place to be out?

Different outdoor places have different precautions and things to be aware of. Search online about how one would stay safe at the places shown below.

Write three tips for keeping safe from each of these different areas:

Area	Three tips for keeping safe
Countryside and parks 	
Towns and cities 	
Roads, railways and transport 	
Sea, lakes and waterways 	

Lesson 3 First aid

Activity 6.3 You in an emergency

What are your reactions like in an emergency? Draw a picture of you in an emergency – you can label it too if you would like to! Afterwards, discuss on what your actions and reaction to an emergency can be with your parent/guardian or a trusted adult.

Unit reflection

Let's revisit key questions from the unit.

What do you know now about keeping yourself safe?

So, are online friends really friends? Explain!

Do you know how to stay safe everywhere? How?

How would you deal with an emergency? Tell us!

Unit 7.7 Changes

What do you know?

- Have you gone through any big changes?
- How does it make you feel?
- What skills have you developed already to deal with change?

In this unit, you will:

- Think about change and how you deal with it.
- Learn that change can be challenging, but life is all about change.
- Understand the value of mistakes.

Lesson 1 Changing zones

Activity 7.1a My pledge to myself

What do we mean by 'comfort zone'? And why do people say that to achieve something, you have to step out of your comfort zone? Discuss this with your parent/guardian and adults in the family.

After your discussion, come up with an aim or a mission that will get you out of your comfort zone. What is your goal? What are you planning to change? How will you know when you have reached it? What new doors will it open up for you?

Use these questions to complete your personal pledge below. Remember to sign and date it at the end.

Lesson 1 Changing zones

Activity 7.1b Advice for my future self

Advice for my future self when I feel I need to step out of my comfort zone again...

- ____________________
- ____________________
- ____________________
- ____________________
- ____________________
- ____________________

Lesson 2 Fall to rise

Activity 7.2a Balance sketches and notes

Use this page to sketch and write notes on the different poses you saw and tried so that you can practise them in the future.

Lesson 2 Fall to rise

Activity 7.2b Reflections on balance

1. What balances did you try? Draw them below.

2. How did you do? Describe your experience and the process of wobbling and falling, and reflect on anything this process has taught you about mistakes.

3. How can you apply what you have learned today to other areas of your life?

Lesson 3 Changing for the better

Activity 7.3a Arguments for each project

Lesson 3 Changing for the better

Activity 7.3b Short-term thinking and long-term thinking

Short-term thinking is when we consider only what is in front of us, such as what we want, or what might happen now or over the next few days or weeks.

Long-term thinking is when we make decisions and consider how a choice we make now will affect people or other things in the future.

If you made your choices imagining the next seven generations were beside you, what sort of decisions might you change?

'Short-term pain, long-term gain' What does this statement mean to you?

How can you apply this statement, and what you have learned about long-term thinking, to your life?

Unit Reflection

How do you feel about change now? Write everything you feel about change in the image below.

Unit 7.8 Yes, we can!

What do you know?

- If you could make one change for the world right now, what would it be?

In this unit, you will:

- Learn how to buy items that help others.
- Improve your environment for wildlife.
- Learn about children's rights.

Lesson 1 Being an ethical consumer

Activity 8.1a Our ethical choices

Read the article below.

Why buy ethically?

Whatever we buy – whether everyday food and goods or bigger purchases such as holidays and cars – there is always a hidden cost. Buying cheap clothes which have been made in sweatshops is a vote for worker exploitation. Buying a gas guzzling 4×4, especially if you are a city dweller, is a vote for climate change. Factory farmed animals, meanwhile, may make cheap meat but it comes at a price on the quality of life of the animal. When it comes to shopping at supermarkets, the cost can be to our high streets and local shops. Even small, everyday purchases, such as coffee, tea, breakfast cereal, bread or bin-bags are a vote for something. Favouring organic produce is a vote for environmental sustainability and Fairtrade is a vote for human rights. As consumers, we have a great deal of power in our pockets. Just look at how the supermarkets and food companies responded on the issue of genetically modified food. Even the threat of withdrawing our custom can change company policy. Considering ethical issues when we go shopping means taking impacts like this into account.

Ethical Consumer website (https://www.ethicalconsumer.org/)

What do you think of this article? Did you know about these issues before or are these new ideas? What do you think about these issues? Talk to your parent/guardian or sibling about this.

Lesson 1 Being an ethical consumer

Activity 8.1b More about our ethical choices

With a friend, reread the article 'Why buy ethically?'.

1. Take each of the items in turn (from 'cheap clothes' to 'Fairtrade') and discuss what good or bad effects on society or the environment you think might result from buying the goods. Note your answers below.

2. Are there any products you do not buy because of your principles or beliefs? If so, what are they and why?

3. Do you know anyone who does not buy certain products or services because of their beliefs? If so, what are they and why?

4. If you could give up something for ethical reasons, what would it be and why?

Lesson 2 Make space for wildlife

Activity 8.2a What would life be like...

If you were a wild animal or insect, what would your life be like if you lived here?

Lesson 2 Make space for wildlife

Activity 8.2b Reflection

Write and draw what you noticed while doing your survey, along with your ideas for improving the neighbourhood's wildlife areas and how you can make this happen.

Lesson 3 Our rights

Activity 8.3a Rights of the Child

Have you heard of the Universal Declaration of Human Rights? Moreover, have you heard about the UN Convention on the Rights of the Child? Sit with an adult and discuss the two ideas. Afterwards, Reflect on what you have learned about the UN Rights of the Child below through notes, writing, drawing or a combination of all of these.

How could you be actively involved in decision-making and take responsibility in your local communities now you understand your rights?

Lesson 3 Our rights

Activity 8.3b My working page

Add photos and/or notes about your learning from this lesson here.

Unit reflection

How are you going to make a difference?

Use this page to write your pledge, big or small, to make the world a better place. Remember to sign it!

Signature	Date

Wellbeing for kids

Making kids smarter, happier

STAGE 8

Hello and welcome to Wellbeing Stage 8!

Changes

Reaching Stage 8 means you are approaching, or have already reached your teens and your body and brain are going through rapid changes – life might possibly feel quite confusing! When this is the case, focusing on your wellbeing and taking really good care of yourself can help a lot.

As you work through the activities and reflections in your workbook, you will learn some brilliant ways to help yourself cope with the challenges the teen years can bring. Here are just a few of the areas this wellbeing workbook will address:

Learn who you are

The activities in your workbook will help you explore who you are, what you like, your identity, your strengths and your values, and what kind of friend you are too. This will help you to feel more confident and have a clearer sense of your identity.

Handling pressure

Social media can be amazing, but it can also make you feel pressured to look a certain way and make you feel bad if you don't. We are going to take a look at body image and self-kindness and learn to appreciate ourselves more.

Self-care

In your teens emotions can feel bigger than ever, but don't worry! From coping with loss, to dealing with anger, there are many useful strategies to help you. Your body also goes through many changes during your teenage years and self-care becomes more and more important.

Family and friends

Is anything more important than your family and friends? Sometimes our relationships with friends and family change, though – how you communicate with them matters hugely, so it is important to think about that and work to improve it!

Learning to look after yourself and the world around you will make you happier and keep you safer. And working through these workbooks will help!

Are you ready to start positively embracing the changes your teen years bring?

May your year be as FANTASTIC as you are!

Becky Goddard-Hill

Unit 8.1 Emotional worlds

What do you know?

- About yourself?
- Ask yourself this question: Who are you?

In this unit, you will:

- Learn about the importance of emotional intelligence.
- Explore how to navigate primary and secondary emotions.
- Understand how, although we all grieve, this can look very different around the world.

Lesson 1 Knowing ourselves

Activity 1.1a Who am I?

Write down all the things that make you, you. This can be a list, a picture with labels or a short piece of writing.

Lesson 1 Knowing ourselves

Activity 1.1b Learning about ourselves

Samirah really didn't like her new teacher. She much preferred Mrs Kumar, who had left last term to teach in a senior class. Samirah's new teacher, Ms Bagul, had asked the class to discuss how we might fall into less pleasant emotions as reactions and Samirah had no clue - and no interest.

"Why don't you just tell us, Ms Bagul?" she asked.

"It is important for the class to think about this and to discuss what this means together, Samirah," Ms Bagul replied.

Samirah had absolutely had enough at this point. She jumped up, tipping her chair to the floor and throwing her pen across the room in anger.

"Ah," Ms Bagul said calmly. "This response demonstrates exactly what this lesson is about, Samirah."

Samirah was startled by what Ms Bagul had said but it made her think. Once she had calmed down, she approached Ms Bagul's desk.

"I'm sorry I got so angry. I just really miss Mrs Kumar's lessons."

"And that response demonstrates a strong awareness of how we can choose to positively react to our emotions, Samirah!"

Samirah's realisation that she was becoming agitated and angry and how she responded afterwards illustrates the difference between allowing your less pleasant feelings to take over, and also becoming aware of when they are building up and taking positive action to manage them.

Now answer the questions on the next page.

1. What do you think Samirah has learned?

2. What do you think is meant by the evaluation at the end of the story?

3. What can you learn from this story?

Lesson 2 Secondary emotions

Activity 1.2 What do we mean by primary and secondary emotions?

Discuss this with your guardian and other adults in your family. After looking at the dictionary for definitions, discuss how secondary emotions can occur. How have you experienced them? Write down your notes below.

Lesson 2 Secondary emotions

Activity 1.2a How to support a friend

Read this extract:

"Gus is always angry, isn't he?" Shola whispered to me as Gus once again got up and stormed out of the class.

It was true that he was always angry... and mean. Most of us kept away from him.

"Can you take this note to the Head of school, please?" Mr Hassan asked me quietly.

"Sure!" I replied.

As I headed down the hallway past the boys' toilets, I heard someone crying. I went in to see if they were OK and was shocked to see it was Gus. He looked so sad.

I froze, waiting for the usual angry response, but instead he said quietly, "I don't know how to get out of this..."

How can you reach out or support your friends in similar situations to Gus's in the future? Note down your ideas below.

Lesson 2 Secondary emotions

Activity 1.2b Reflections

Write the 'top tips to find the language of your emotions' here.

Now write anything else you have learned below.

Ask yourself, 'How can this new awareness of secondary emotions help me now and in the future?'

Lesson 3 Celebrating and mourning a life

Activity 1.3 Traditions

You are learning about how different people celebrate and mourn when people die.

First, with an adult, watch this TED Talk online: Kelli Swazey – 'Life that doesn't end with death'. Ask questions if you have any and discuss the video with your parent/guardian. Below, write and/or draw your family's and your culture's traditions around death. For example, how does your family or culture mourn? What are your family customs/rituals? For how long? Do you wear any special clothes or eat any special food?

Unit reflection

If you could see emotions, what would they look like? There is no right or wrong here – grab some colours and draw what you feel. You can annotate the page with what you have learned or wish to know more about.

Unit 8.2 Caring for you, caring for me

What do you know?

- What do you understand about wellbeing?
- Why might this image relate to wellbeing?

In this unit, you will:

- Learn about how to change the narrative on body image.
- Learn how to spread kindness, to yourself and others.
- Learn how you can do something simple and enjoyable that will look after your emotional self-care.

Lesson 1 Body image

Activity 2.1a Adverts

Cut out two fashion adverts (with models) that you like and glue them on to this page.

Now write down what it is that you like about these images, the models and the clothes.

Lesson 1 Body image

Activity 2.1b The Body in History.

Throughout history, people have had different ideas of what makes a body perfect or attractive. Take a look at some of the ideas that would be considered odd today. You can try looking up images online for the same.

1. In Ancient Greece, men had a lot of pressure upon themselves to look almost perfect. This was held up with the belief that physical looks reflect one's intelligence.
2. In Renaissance Italy, women were expected to be full-bodied and blonde in order to reflect the status of the family. Their behaviour was also expected to be quiet and shy.
3. The 18th century saw the arrival of make-up in Europe, and things like blushes and whitened faces became fashionable. Often, the addition of a fake mole or beauty spot was also encouraged.
4. In Victorian England, women were expected to be full-bodied, but at the same time, wear corsets which restricted their movement and comfort to give the appearance of an 'hour-glass' figure.
5. In the 1920s, short hair and a thin frame became the go-to look for women across Europe.
6. While earlier men were expected to simply be in good health and physically athletic, in the 90s and the years following it, the ideal body for men became one that was muscular, with huge biceps and six-pack abs. Whether the person was athletic or even in good health was besides the point.

Discuss these different ideas of physical attractiveness with your parent/guardian, and ask them what body ideals existed during their youth.

Lesson 1 Body image

Activity 2.1b What have you learned?

Use this page to write up what you have found out about body image through history or how people with obvious physical differences accept the body they are in.

What have you learned from this research?

Lesson 2 Kindness

Activity 2.2a Your own worst enemy

What do you think this quote means?

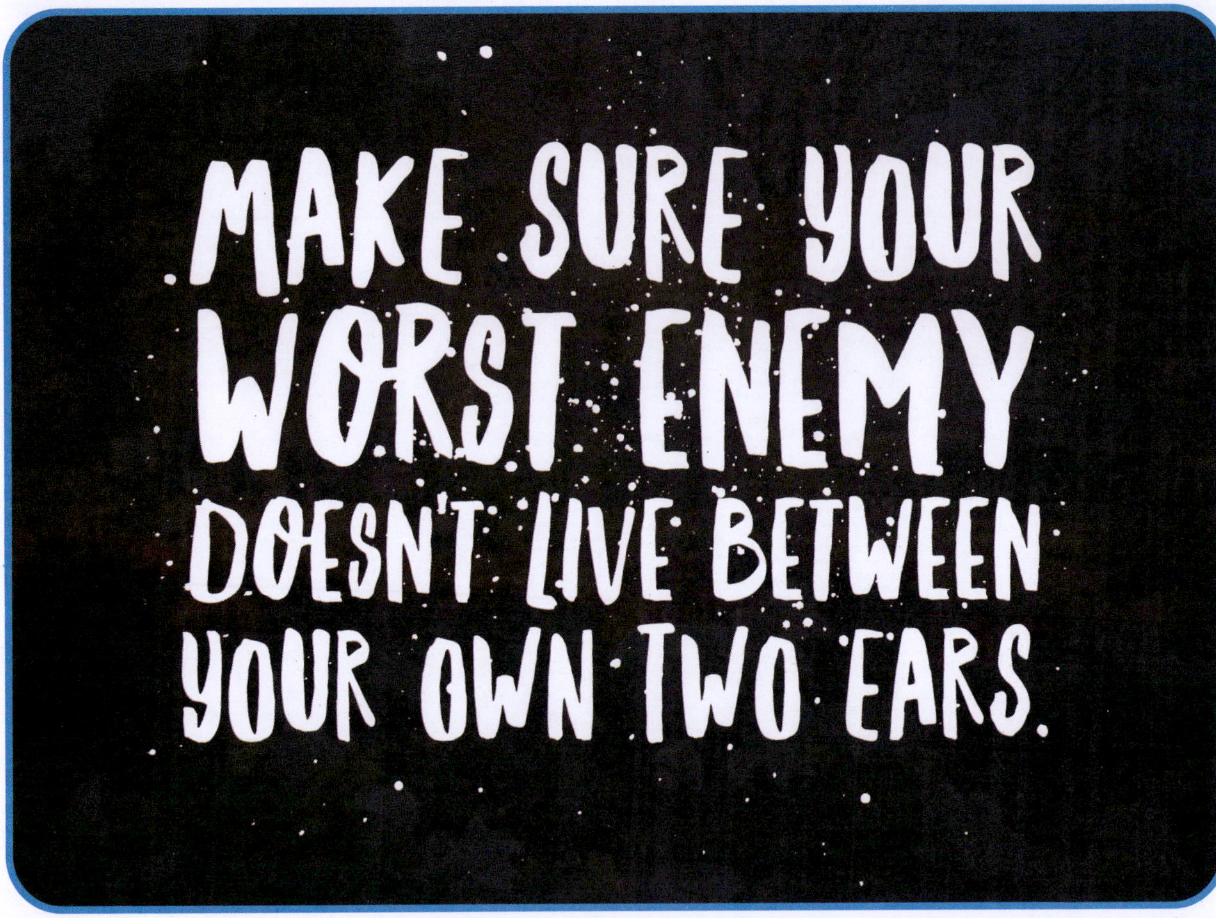

Lesson 2 Kindness

Activity 2.2b The Kindness Ripple

What do you think 'The Ripple Effect' means? Just like a small disturbance in a pool of water results in ripples going farther and farther away, the same way, a small act on our part can affect other people and things. And what if your action is that of kindness? What kind of ripples would it produce? Discuss with your parent/guardian and then watch a video on 'The Science of Kindness' by Random Acts of Kindness Foundation.

Lesson 2 Kindness

Activity 2.2b Video planning notes

After watching the video on kindness, it is time to make your own short film on being kind! Ask your friends and family members to participate in it and get their suggestions on it too. Use this sheet to plan your video. Remember, this is a short film, so it will need careful planning for it to run smoothly.

How long will the film be? ____________________

What acts of kindness are going to be happening in your film?

____

____

Is anyone talking, or is it silent or with a voiceover by a narrator? ____________________

____

____

Who is doing the filming/acting? ____________________

____

____

Where will you do the filming? ____________________

____

____

What will you need? ____________________

____

____

____

Lesson 2 Kindness

Activity 2.2c Self-talk

How can you change negative self-talk into positive self-talk using the information you have learned in this lesson? Write or draw your ideas below.

Lesson 3 Emotional self-care

Activity 2.3 'Me time'

What does 'me time' mean to you?

Draw or write what you like to do in your 'me time'!

Unit reflection

Imagine you are writing a speech about body image, kindness and self-care (everything you have learned in this unit!). What would you say to inspire people to be kind to themselves and others about these aspects of their personal lives?

wisdom

Try writing your speech below. Add at least one important point from each lesson and imagine you have a huge crowd of adoring fans in front of you desperate to hear you share your wisdom.

Unit 8.3 Healthy bodies

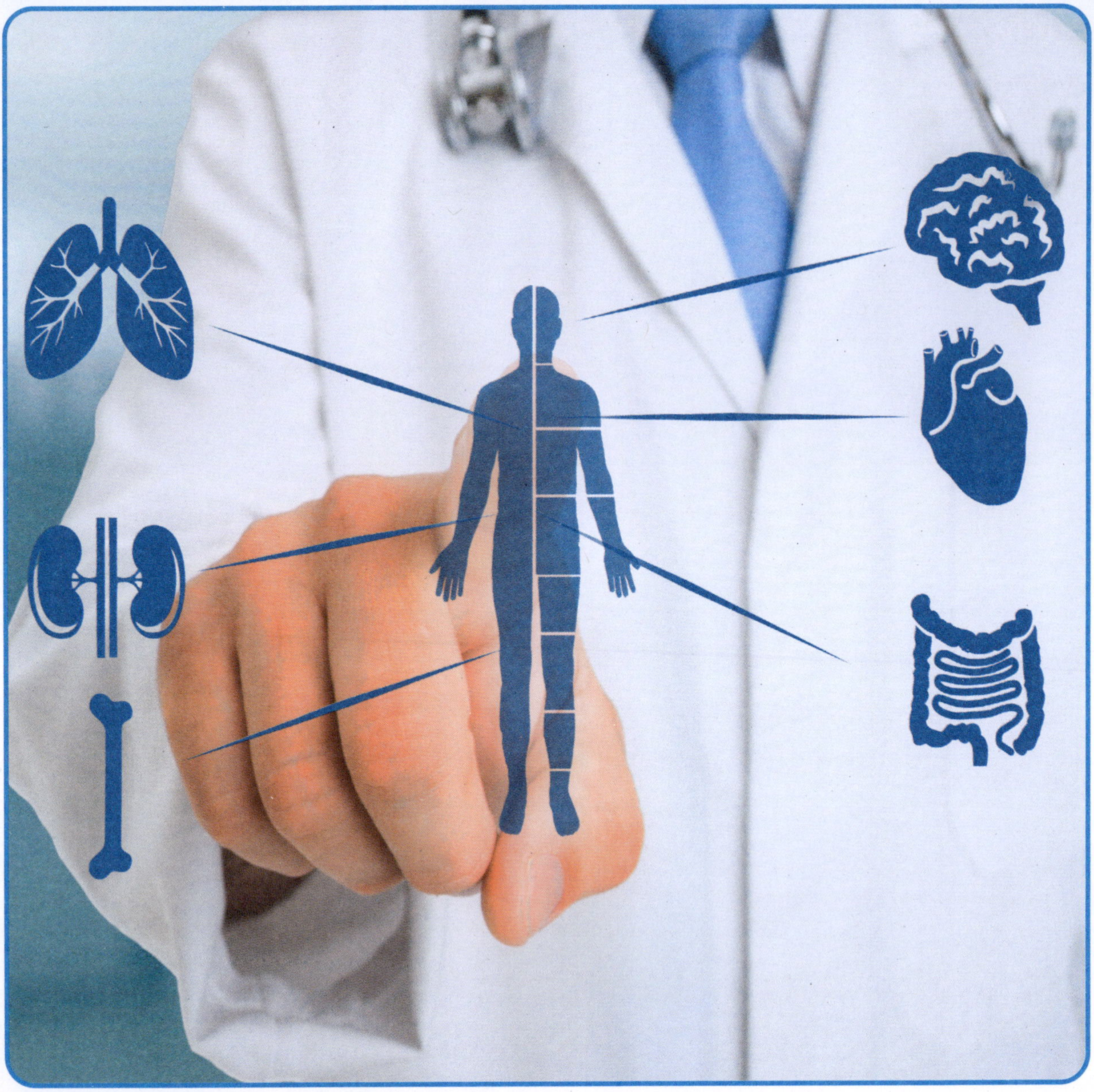

What do you know?

- About healthy habits?

In this unit, you will:

- Learn about preventative healthcare.
- Understand how to keep your cardiovascular system and joints healthy.
- Explore what to do with oily skin and hair.

Lesson 1 Preventative healthcare

Activity 3.1a What do you know?

Have you heard of the saying 'Prevention is better than cure'? Preventative healthcare includes several different measures and methods that help us stay fit and keeps all kinds of infectious diseases at bay. Vaccines, immunisations, health checks, self-examination – what do you know? What have you heard of? Write everything you can think of in the syringe below and discuss and find out more methods with the help of your parent/guardian.

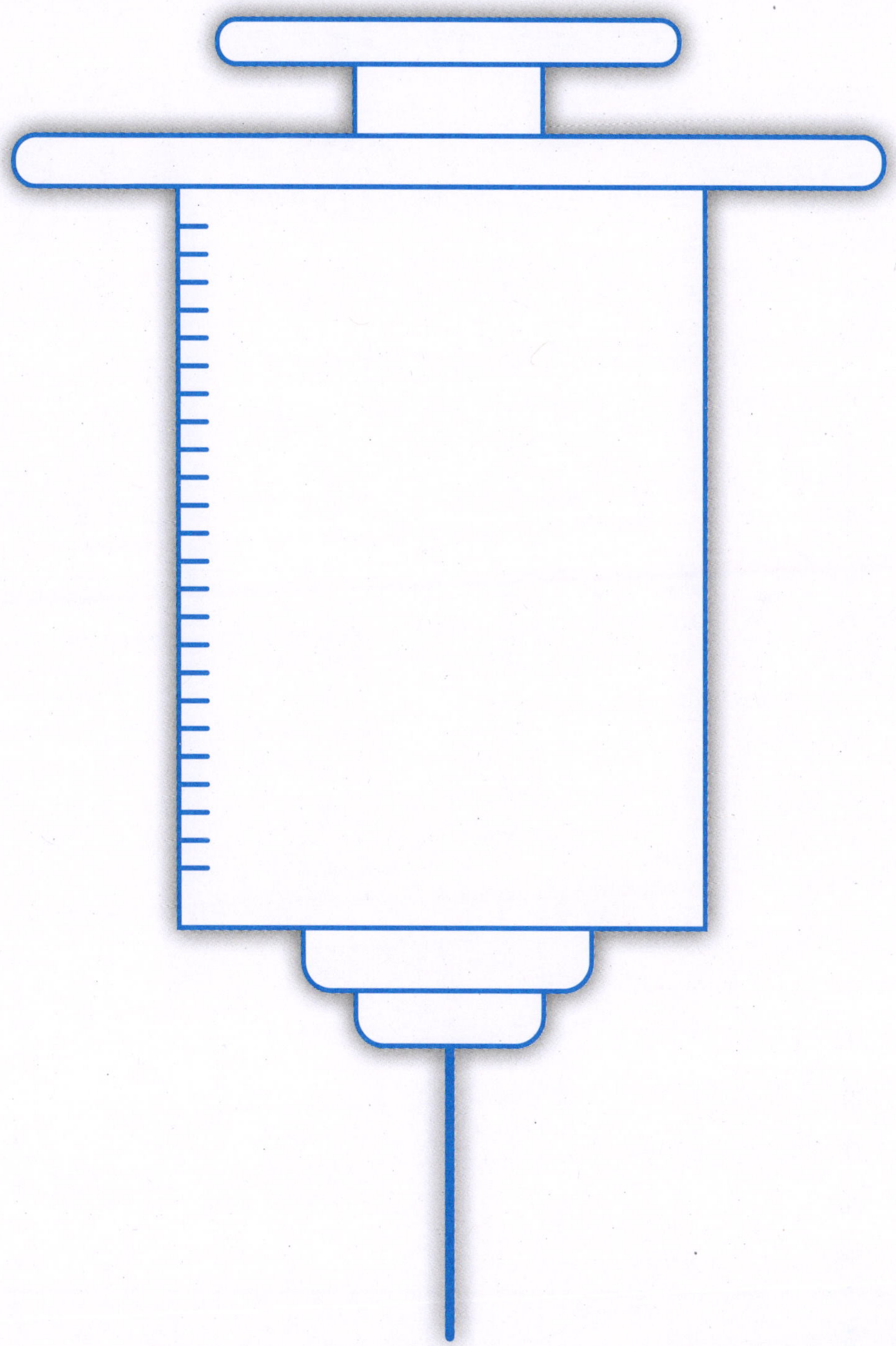

Lesson 1 Preventative healthcare

Activity 3.1b What I now know about preventative healthcare

Write or draw what you have learned and how you can use this information to look after your health as you grow.

Lesson 2 Exercise to health

Activity 3.2a Joints

Scan the body below and circle places where you think there is a joint. Following this, discuss with your parent/guardian about joints and check whether there are any joints you missed on marking.

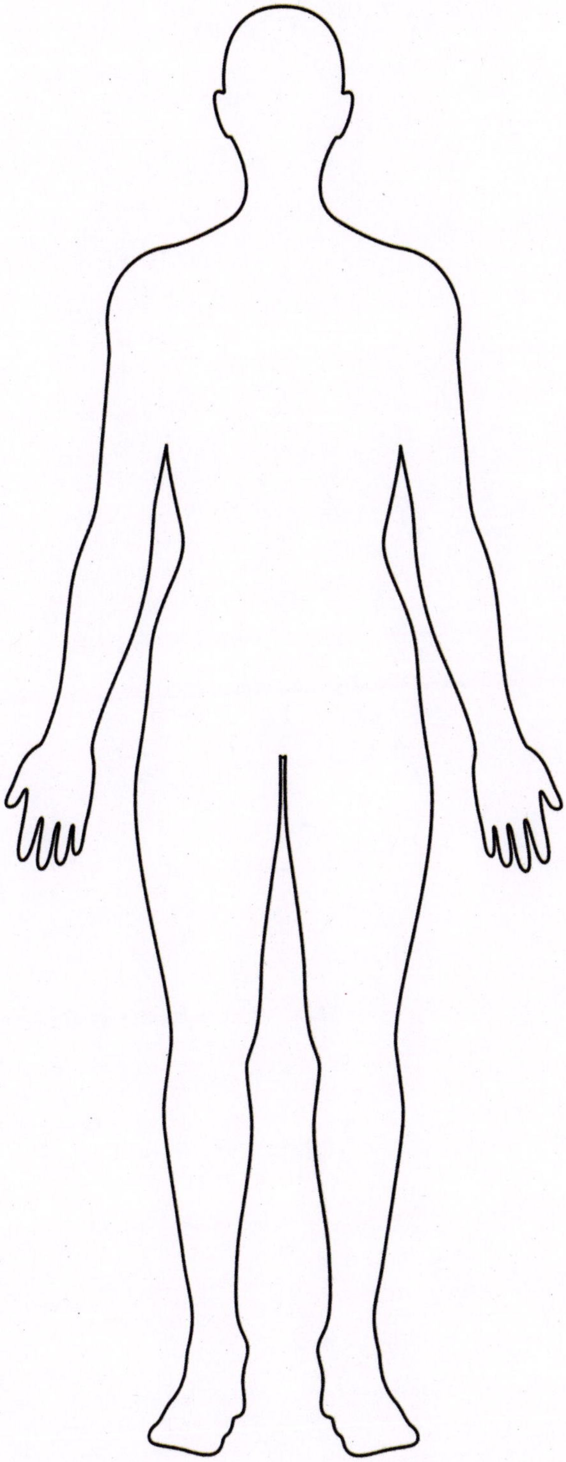

Lesson 2 Exercise to health

Activity 3.2b Getting more exercise

My promise to myself (that my future self will thank me for!)

I promise ...

Lesson 3 Looking after our skin

Activity 3.3a How to deal with acne

Read the advice below and then draw a cartoon strip using the boxes to show how to deal with acne; include each numbered point in a different box.

1. Wash your face twice a day with lukewarm water and a mild soap.
2. Don't wash it more than that as you may irritate the skin and make it worse.
3. Do not squeeze spots. This can make them worse and can result in permanent scarring.
4. Avoid using make-up to hide spots. (Choose water-based make-up when you do.)
5. Ask your doctor or pharmacist for advice on which creams to use.
6. If your acne is severe, you may need to see your doctor and have a course of treatment.

Lesson 3 Looking after our skin

Activity 3.3b Top tips for healthy teeth

Like skin, another area of our body that needs to be regularly looked after and taken care of is our teeth. You must already be aware of brushing one's teeth twice a day. What other tips do you know? Discuss them with your parent/guardian. Write all the tips you can think of around this illustration – you can use it to help you remember everything.

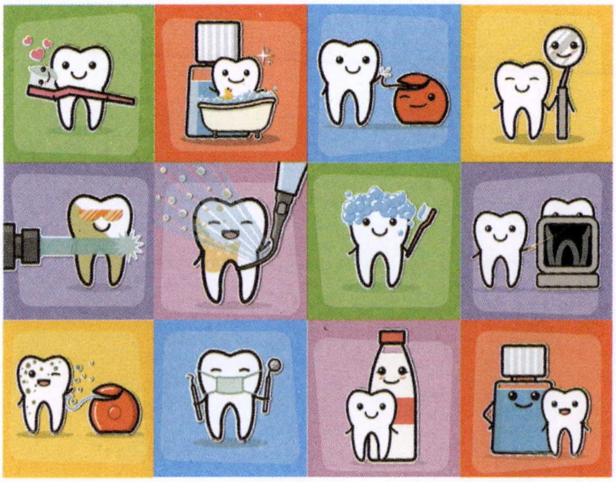

Unit reflection

What have you learned in this unit? Consider three things you have learned in each lesson and draw them in the film reels below.

1. What have you learned about preventative healthcare?

2. What have you learned about how exercise can support cardiovascular and joint health?

3. What have you learned about how to manage your own personal hygiene?

Unit 8.4 Positive communication

What do you know?

- Think about yourself as a friend and family member. How well do you listen? Do you have arguments? Do they get resolved? How do you communicate?

In this unit, you will:

- Learn how to listen actively.
- Consider how to deal appropriately with anger and how to resolve arguments better.
- Understand how to become more connected with those you spend your days with.

Lesson 1 Active listening

Activity 4.1a How well were you listening?

Pair up with a friend and tell each other a story. It can be anything, real or imaginary. After both of you have told your stories, without asking any clarifying questions, write it down below, remembering as much detail as you can. When you have finished you will show your partner your work and they will show you theirs, to see how much you remembered.

This will give you a clear insight into how well you were listening! You can add a comment below about how well you think you did and mark your listening skills out of 10 if you would like to.

Lesson 1 Active listening

Activity 4.1b Active listening skills

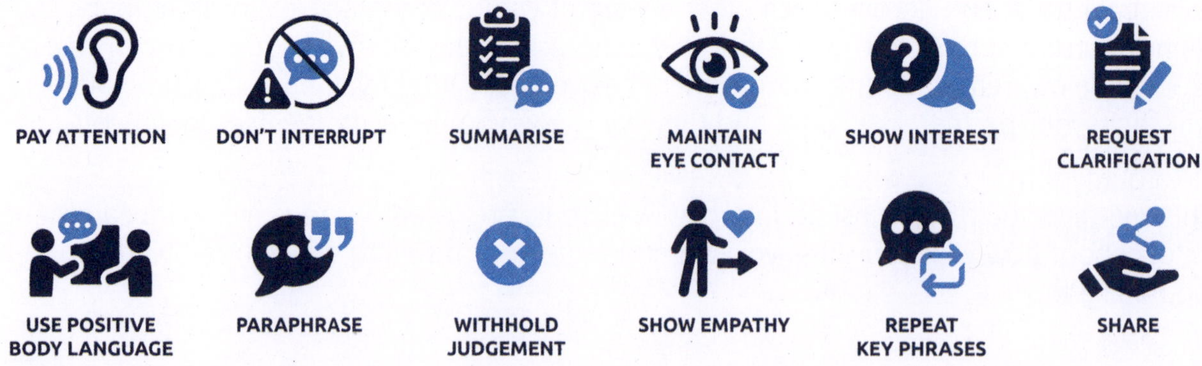

- ✓ Pay attention – Don't fidget or look around; stay focused on the person talking.
- ✓ Don't interrupt – Wait until the person has finished speaking before you say something.
- ✓ Summarise – Use expressions like 'so, what you are saying is...' or 'what happened is...'.
- ✓ Maintain eye contact – Don't stare, but keep your eyes on theirs and show that you are engaged.
- ✓ Show interest – You can do this by nodding, smiling, and saying things like 'tell me more' or 'that sounds so good', 'I know what you mean', 'I understand'.
- ✓ Request clarification – Ask questions to make sure you have understood correctly.
- ✓ Use positive body language – Lean forward, nod, don't have your arms crossed.
- ✓ Paraphrase – Repeat what they have said in less detail to make sure you are listening well.
- ✓ Without judgement – Don't assume. Don't judge until you have really listened and understood what they are saying.
- ✓ Show empathy – If they are sharing something personal or difficult or that you don't understand, try to imagine how they must feel.
- ✓ Repeat key phrases – You can say things like 'she said...' or 'then you did...' and repeat what they have said.
- ✓ Share – Identify with what they are saying by talking about your own experiences or thoughts when they have finished.

Lesson 2 Dealing with anger

Activity 4.2a What do you do when you get angry?

Sometimes we find ourselves angry when we are in an argument. There is a saying: 'It takes two people to argue – one to start it and one to finish it.'

If you have lost your temper, you are likely to say things that you don't mean and not respond rationally to what is going on. The best thing to do is to stop the argument, let both of you calm down, and then continue the discussion later.

Here are some examples of ways to do this:

✓ Take slow deep breaths before acting or reacting.

✓ Leave the room or go to the toilet. This creates a break in proceedings.

✓ Walk away calmly, ignoring negative comments from the other person.

✓ Tell the other person that you can't discuss things now, but will talk to them again later when you're calmer.

1. Circle the ideas you think could or do help you.

2. Do you have or know of any other techniques to deal with anger? List these below.

3. Talk about these techniques with your parent/guardian and write down any others they suggest that you think might help you.

Lesson 2 Dealing with anger

Activity 4.2b What to do after an argument

After an argument, it is important to recognise how you feel. If the argument was with a friend, sibling or suggest, it is important to make up. You should:

- ✓ Apologise for the part you played, regardless of whether or not the other person was wrong. Say, 'I'm sorry' rather than, 'I'm sorry but ...'. Adding a 'but' risks continuing the argument.
- ✓ Listen carefully to what the other person is saying. There is always more than one perspective in a situation. You may have missed something important they said.
- ✓ Analyse what really happened. This is because there are actually three perspectives in any situation – your perspective, that of the person you were arguing with, and what really happened. It can be useful to discuss what happened with an independent third person.
- ✓ Treat the situation as a learning experience. We can't change other people's behaviour, but we can change our own. There is always room to learn. Ask yourself what you would do differently next time.
- ✓ Even if you have not resolved the situation, put it behind you. It is better for you and your health to just let it go.
- ✓ If something is still bothering you after an argument, apply the five-year rule to it: think, will it still be bothering you in five years' time? If not, it is time to let it go.

1. Circle the ideas you think could or do help you.

2. Do you have or know of any other useful things to do or say after an argument? List these below.

____

____

____

____

3. Talk about these techniques with your partner and write down any others they suggest that you think might help you.

____

____

____

____

Lesson 2 Dealing with anger

Activity 4.2c My anger strategy

How can you respectfully articulate (express) your thoughts when they are different from those of others, without getting angry? Write or draw your ideas here, thinking about what you have learned in this lesson.

Lesson 3 Getting more connected

Activity 4.3 Two truths and a lie

It's time for a group game! Gather a few of your friends or classmates, and with them, play a game of two truths and a lie. A person will step forward and say two truths and one lie about themselves. The rest of the group has to figure out which statement is the lie. Use this page to write down some truths and lies about yourself that you can use for this game. Don't label which is which until the game has finished as someone might see them!

Unit reflection

Write down everything you have learned in this unit. You have 2 minutes. Go!

Unit 8.5 Friends and family

What do you know?

- How have you changed in your life so far?
- How have your changes since you were a baby affected people around you?

In this unit, you will:

- Explore how friendships change over time.
- Learn about family traditions.
- Consider how a family changes.

Lesson 1 Friends

Activity 5.1a Your friends

How many different sorts of friendships do you have (e.g. at school, clubs, neighbours)?

What are your favourite sorts of friendships? (Ones where you can talk about deep things? Have a laugh? Do active stuff together?)

Draw your best friends here:

Lesson 1 Friends

Activity 5.1b My friends in the future

It's time to take a peek into the future! Do a visualisation exercise about who you will be in the future. Sit comfortably and close your eyes, relax your body and try to clear your mind. If a thought comes in, just push it aside. Focus on your slow breathing for a count of three in and three out. Imagine yourself as an older person. See in your mind's eye what you are wearing, where you are living, and what sorts of friends you have. Can they visualise any friends? How many are there? How are you spending your time together as friends? After about 3–5 minutes of visualising, bring your focus back to your breath, become aware of your surroundings and then slowly open your eyes. In case you need help, get an adult family member to participate. Sketch and label everything you visualised in the cloud below.

Lesson 2 Family traditions

Activity 5.2a Current traditions

What family traditions do you have each week, each month or each year? Write or draw all the different traditions you have in the space below. They can be as small as what you eat on a certain day or what you say when someone sneezes, to as big as what happens at a family wedding or on a holy day.

Lesson 2 Family traditions

Activity 5.2b Future traditions

- Which traditions are your favourites and why?

- Which traditions would you like to keep going when you are an adult and why?

- Which traditions might you like to drop or add?

Lesson 3 Families

Activity 5.3a What's important to you?

Look at the following list. Decide which of these is important in a family. Then rate the statement according to how important you think it is, on a scale of 1 to 5, where 1 is not important and 5 is the most important. Give reasons for your views.

Situation	Important? (yes/no)	How important? (1 to 5)	Reason
Having love and affection			
Having lots of nice things bought for you			
Having a safe space to live			
Having people around you who support you and 'have your back'			
Having people to teach and guide you, and to push you to be the best you can be			
Having fun and enjoying each other's company			
Having people to talk to about things that worry you or that you need help with			
Having someone who cleans your clothes and feeds you			

What other aspects of family life are important to you? Why are they important?

____

____

____

Lesson 3 Families

Activity 5.3b Zooming forward

You have done a visualisation where you zoomed 20 years into the future. Now use these questions to write down how you think your family life might look 20 years from now. Remember, this might not happen, but you are using your imagination to try and guess!

1. Where will you be living?

____

____

____

2. Who will you be living with?

____

____

____

3. Will you be a parent? If so, what sort of parent will you be and why?

____

____

____

4. What sort of a family unit will you have and why?

____

____

____

Use this space to add anything else you 'saw' in your family life visualisation.

Unit reflection

Look back over this unit. What have you learned? Draw some of the key learning points below.

What would you like to know more about?

Unit 8.6 Knowledge is power

What do you know about:

- Looking after yourself online?
- Looking after yourself around strangers?
- Looking after yourself if the weather becomes extreme?

In this unit, you will learn:

- What to do during extreme weather.
- How to stay safe when interacting with strangers.
- How to post and share safely online.

Lesson 1 Strangers

Activity 6.1a Thinking about safety

What's happening here?

What do you think they would need to think about in terms of their safety and why? Discuss with your parent/guardian before making notes below.

Lesson 1 Strangers

Activity 6.1b The golden rule

As seen in the page before and in your discussion, there are several things to think about while being safe at home and outdoors. This doesn't mean one should be scared of going out, but there are just a few things that one needs to take into account. And the golden rule for going out with friends is always 'Leave together, come home together'. Sticking together ensures not just your own safety, but that of your friends and loved ones too.

Write the golden rule below in an interesting style and decorate the page to make it memorable.

Golden rule

Lesson 2 Extreme weather

Activity 6.2 Extreme weather event

Your extreme weather event is: ______________________________

____

Your report needs to include:

- A brief explanation of the extreme weather event.
- The effects of this extreme weather event.
- What people can do to prepare.
- What people should do to keep safe.

Write your report below and on the following page, making sure you cover these points.

____

____

____

____

____

____

____

____

____

____

____

____

____

____

____

____

____

____

____

____

____

Lesson 3 Sharing online

Activity 6.3a Online posts

What do you post online or share with friends or family via sites or chat/texts? Write and/or draw the different sites and apps you use and the places you go online and then add what sorts of things you like to share or post on them.

Lesson 3 Sharing online

Activity 6.3b Being present in your life

What do you think of this?

Unit reflection

This unit is called 'Knowledge is power'. How can what you have learned in these three lessons give you power?

Unit 8.7 Changes and choices

What do you know?

- What might be happening with the person in the photo?
- How does she look like she is feeling about that?

In this unit, you will:

- Learn how to navigate changes.
- Understand how to make the most of mistakes.
- Consider what choices are available to you.

Lesson 1 Changes and emotions

Activity 7.1a Changes, mistakes and choices

When things are changing, how do you feel? When you make mistakes, how does it affect you? When you are given lots of choices, how do you cope?

Consider the statements below. Put a tick beside the ones that apply to you. When you have finished, share your responses with an adult family member and discuss what they tell you about your personality.

1. I find it really hard when I make mistakes.	
2. I am happy to ask for help.	
3. I like to be honest and talk about how I feel.	
4. I am excited by new challenges.	
5. I am very nervous when I have to do something new.	
6. I am willing to take risks.	
7. I am very cautious.	
8. I get overwhelmed if I have too many choices.	
9. I see mistakes as a chance to learn.	
10. I find life an adventure.	

What does this tell you about your personality?

Lesson 1 Changes and emotions

Activity 7.1b Positives and negatives of change

Change is always complex. With five family members or friends, split yourselves up into two teams of three. One team will be 'Team positive' while the other will be 'Team negative'. The first team will try finding out and listing the positive aspects of changes, while the other team will list the negative features about changes. Write both in the lists below and discuss each of them. Write your team's ideas below and when the other team is giving their feedback write down their ideas too.

Team positives	Team negatives

Which do you agree with most? (Or do you feel the emotions around change are equal?) Write your thoughts here, explaining why you feel the way you do about change.

____

____

____

____

____

Lesson 2 Handling mistakes

Activity 7.2a What's happening here?

Write down what is happening in this picture in as much detail as you can.

Lesson 2 Handling mistakes

Activity 7.2b The value of mistakes

- Embrace your humanness!
- Remaining teachable and open to learning will get you much further than being closed-minded and unteachable.
- There is no one in the world who hasn't made a mistake.
- Some 'mistakes' have led to the discovery of DNA, penicillin, aspirin and X-rays!

Lesson 3 Next steps

Activity 7.3a What's happening here?

Write down below what you think is happening? Has it ever happened with you too? How did you feel?

Lesson 3 Next steps

Activity 7.3b Small steps reach goals

Looking into our future as taking big steps can feel overwhelming, but if we break it down into little steps, our goals will be more easily achievable. When we map out our goals and focus on small achievable, 'tickable' daily steps, this will help us achieve them. Think of them like steps on a ladder, which you're taking to get to the top. Find out a long term goal that you would like to achieve, and discuss with your parent/guardian how you can get started with little steps. Use the ladder below to work out and write down the small steps you will need to reach your goal. You can use two ladders if you have two goals or are just thinking about different ideas at the moment and want to compare them.

Unit reflection

Use this page to create a mind map of all the things you want to change and the choices you want to make!

Unit 8.8 Be the change

What do you know?

- If you ruled the world, what would you do to make it a fairer, kinder place?

In this unit, you will:

- Find ways to help build a kinder, fairer world.
- Devise an action plan to environmentally improve your local area.
- Do your bit to get involved with local communities and projects.

Lesson 1 Standing up for each other

Activity 8.1a Is this justice?

Look at the symbolism of the image. Is this justice? Write your thoughts and explain your answer.

What is already being done in the world/your country to create a fairer, kinder world for everyone?

Lesson 1 Standing up for each other

Activity 8.1b You see a hateful post online

Hate speech is when a group of people or an individual are attacked for their characteristics – these are things that the person cannot change. This sort of abuse is extremely distressing to the individual and in some countries it is also illegal. Discuss it and why people do it with your parent/guardian.

Now imagine that someone has put up a hateful post online. What choices do you have? What do you need to do? Recall all that you have learned and discussed and write the steps you would need to take below.

Lesson 2 Eco action

Activity 8.2a Local issues

Look at the images on the right. What do you think they show? And how does it make you feel? What concerns do you have in the local area? Are there any similar local concerns you might have?

Lesson 2 Eco action

Activity 8.2b Planning page

With your guardian or a trusted adult, go through the latest environmental headlines in your local newspapers and news outlets. Discuss the various issues and pick one up that you would like to do something about. Then, with a mix of friends and family members, plan a project regarding it and what you can do to solve the problem to some extent. Use this page to plan your project for how you are going to protect or improve your local environment.

Lesson 3 Our school council

Activity 8.3a

What do you remember about the UN Rights of the Child? Create a mind map of everything you know and remember from previous lessons.

UN Rights of the Child

Lesson 3 Our school council

Activity 8.3b Our plans

A school council is set up as a formal team of students who represent their class and other students in the school, so that children can be actively involved in decision-making and become responsible. Members of a school council are elected by their school mates and take the role for a year before the council is re-elected. During that year, the council meets regularly to raise issues that concern students across various areas, be it studies, sports facilities, timetables, or libraries. Do some research to learn about how school councils run. For example, how will you set up elections? What will your roles and responsibilities be? What will your action plan be? In case your school does not have a council, you can start one up! With the action plan you write below, invite your school principal and class teacher to initiate the process.

Unit reflection

How can you 'be the change'? Write all your ideas below.

Wellbeing for kids

Making kids smarter, happier

STAGE 9

Hello and welcome to Wellbeing Stage 9!

You are getting smarter all the time (that's why your school work is getting harder!). This means that you are ready to handle more complex emotional wellbeing issues, and the activities in this workbook will help you learn and practise these.

Some of the areas looked at in this workbook include:

Relationships and communication

You will discover how to use non-verbal communication and how to build empathy. These skills will help you so much in all your relationships.

Empathy not only helps in your relationships with family and friends, but it also helps you notice and challenge discrimination and helps you to become a better ally.

Keeping safe

You will also address some serious issues this year, including cyberbullying, risky behaviour and personal boundaries. These can all have such a huge impact on your life and knowing how to keep safe in all these areas is vitally important if you want to stay happy and healthy.

Perfectly imperfect

Life can be messy, and things do go wrong sometimes and that's okay. It's all part of being human. We need to embrace and learn from mistakes and build up resilience, rather than focusing on perfectionism. The activities in this book will show you how! They will also help you become a GREAT problem solver, which is a wonderful skill to have. It will prevent you feeling stuck or overwhelmed and help you to move forward positively.

There are so many helpful things to learn about wellbeing that can help you to help yourself. Let's make a start...

This is your year to SHINE!

Becky Goddard-Hill

Unit 9.1 Understanding others

What do you know?

- What actions or feelings could have happened to make two people shake hands?
- What do you do to try to understand other people?

In this unit, you will:

- Learn about non-verbal communication.
- Understand what empathy is and how to build it in yourself.
- Recognise how people grieve differently.

Lesson 1 Non-verbal communication

Activity 1.1a Challenge script

Write a short script with your friends, about someone going into a shop to buy some food. They drop some food by accident and it spills and makes a huge mess. The shop assistant comes out to clean it up. Then they accidentally jump the queue and someone shouts at them.

Your challenge when acting it out is to have conflicting verbal and non-verbal communication! Can you achieve it?

Script

Characters

Stage direction

Script

Lesson 1 Non-verbal communication

Activity 1.1b How did you find the challenge script?

Explain the opposing emotions you chose and how you and your friends showed this opposing verbal and non-verbal communication in your scripts and acting.

Lesson 2 Building empathy

Activity 1.2a Interview questions

Building empathy is imagining how you would feel in situations you see other people in and showing that you see them and recognise what they are going through, or at least try to understand, even if it is not in your direct experience (e.g. a homeless person). To practise empathy, you can try asking yourself, 'Imagine if that was me. How would I feel?'

Here's an exercise in being empathetic that you would find interesting. Pick a friend you are still getting to know. Ask them these questions and note down what they say.

1. What do you enjoy doing? ____________________

____

2. How would you describe the sort of person you are? ____________________

____

3. What's your most common saying? ____________________

____

4. What's your favourite subject at school? ____________________

____

5. What's your favourite food? ____________________

____

6. What is something I don't know about you? ____________________

____

7. What are your favourite colours? ____________________

____

8. What makes you happy? ____________________

____

9. What makes you sad? ____________________

____

10. Is there anything else you want to tell me?

____

____

Lesson 2 Building empathy

Activity 1.2b Portrait

Now that you have interviewed your friend, using the information in the interview, create their portrait! Use lots of colours and empathy to create it. Remember, it doesn't need to have perfect resemblance, just the essence of the person you have gotten to know. Stick a photo of your finished portrait here and annotate it to show why you chose to add the things you did in the style you did.

Has this activity developed your empathy? If so, how?

Lesson 3 Grief and loss

Activity 1.3a The grief and loss cycle

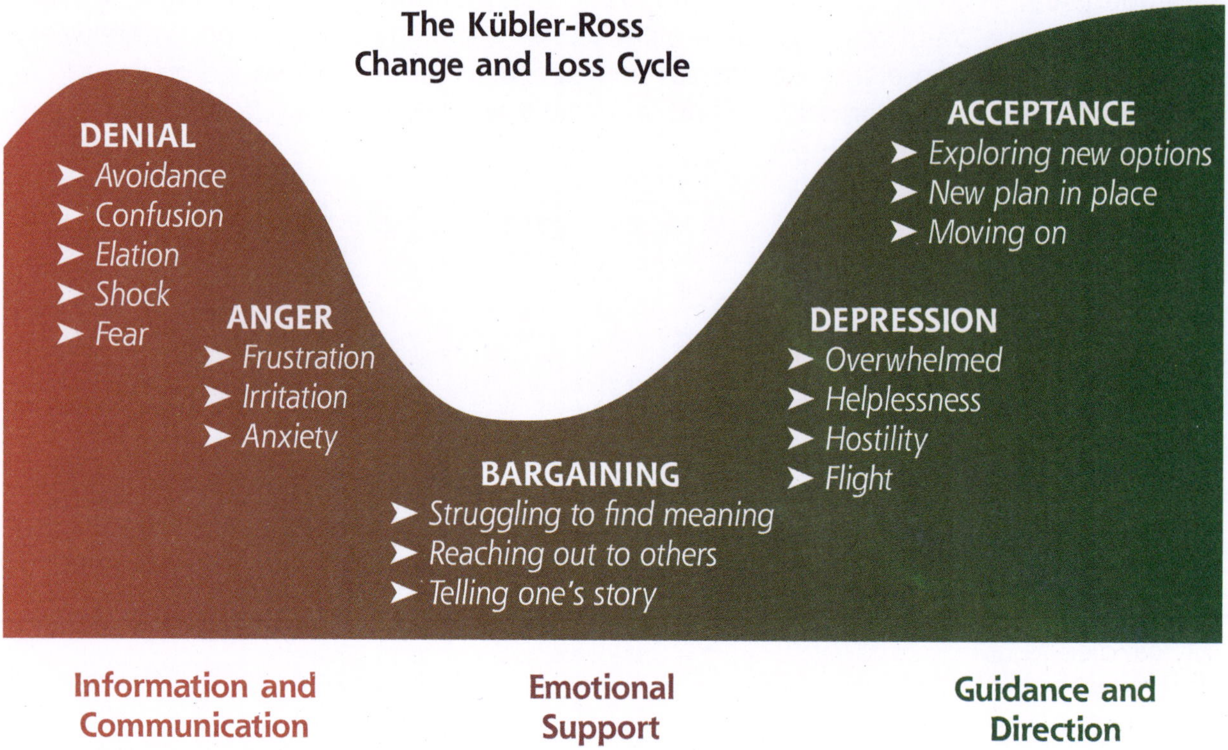

The five stages of grief

1. **Denial:** The stage of shock or denial is usually the first stage in the Kübler-Ross model and is mostly short-lived. This is a phase when someone might take time to process their loss or grief.

2. **Anger:** When the realisation finally hits, someone might become angry and may look for someone to blame. Anger can be expressed in many ways.

3. **Bargaining:** When the stage of anger passes, someone may start thinking about ways to postpone the inevitable and try to find out the best thing left in the situation.

4. **Depression:** This is a stage when someone tends to feel sadness, fear, regret, guilt and other negative emotions.

5. **Acceptance:** When people realise that fighting the change that is coming into their life is not going to make the grief go away, they accept it completely even though it still hurts.

Lesson 3 Grief and loss

Activity 1.3b The five stages of grief

It is important to understand that we do not move along the stages in a neat line. A person tends to move into stages in a random order and may sometimes even return to a previous stage after a certain point in time. Each stage can last for a different length of time, and it is possible for a person to get stuck in a particular stage and not move on from there. Discuss these stages and the grief cycle with your parent/guardian.

Complete the table below, considering where you think each person is in their grief cycle. Then write down how you think they could help themselves. (Scenario one has been done for you.)

Scenario	Stage	How could this person help themselves?
Ever since my grandad died I feel so cross with everyone. Why didn't my parents take us to see him more often? Why didn't the carers in his care home help him more?	Anger	They could go to their doctor and find a counsellor or a therapist to get some support with their feelings and help them find some acceptance.
My cat died today. I've had her for 15 years. She just collapsed. I know I should feel sad, but I don't feel anything. What's wrong with me? I'm feeling so confused.		
A few years ago my friend died. After it happened, I got so depressed. My friends and family have been so supportive, I don't know what I'd do without them. Today I feel good, at peace.		
My best friend is from New Zealand and has to move back in a few months. I can't imagine life without her – we've been friends forever. I'm crying at the littlest things. My life feels like it's over.		
My big brother and I are really close. He tells me he's planning on going travelling for a year. I'm so worried he won't come home. I spent hours trying to convince him to change his mind or let me go with him.		

Unit reflection

Look back over this unit. What are the two main points from each lesson? Write them below.

Non-verbal communication

1. ____________________

____

____

2. ____________________

____

____

Building empathy

1. ____________________

____

____

2. ____________________

____

____

Grief and loss

1. ____________________

____

____

2. ____________________

____

____

Unit 9.2 Choosing kindness

What do you know?

- How can we choose kindness?
- List some of the places or situations we could be more kind.

In this unit, you will:

- Learn about self-esteem through finding strengths.
- Understand cyberbullying.
- Find balance in our lives.

Lesson 1 Let's Shine!

Activity 2.1 Self-esteem and self-image

Two phrases that are connected to our confidence and how we interact with the world are self-esteem and self-image. Self-esteem is how we view and judge ourselves. It is based on who we think we are and over time, these thoughts can turn into personal beliefs. Self image is a similar concept where we have a mental image of our physical selves, that is mixed with things we have heard about ourselves. It is therefore able to be affected by how other's see us and think of us, no matter how confident we might be.

As an activity, pick a classmate or an acquaintance you know is kind but who you do not know that well. Have them write about all the positive things, both inside and out, about you, and do the same for them.

Lesson 1 Let's shine!

Activity 2.1a Reflection

You have just done an activity to consider whether your self-image is the same as the image others have of you. Using what your partner has written, answer the questions below independently, spending some time to reflect quietly on this experience and what you can take from it.

1. What did your partner say about your strengths and the positive things they see about you? ____________________

____

____

____

2. Were you surprised about what your partner saw in you? Why? ____________________

____

____

____

____

3. Has it made you question anything you thought about yourself? Explain. ____________________

____

____

____

____

____

4. How can you build on this experience to re-evaluate your self-image and self-esteem?

____

____

____

____

____

Lesson 1 Let's shine!

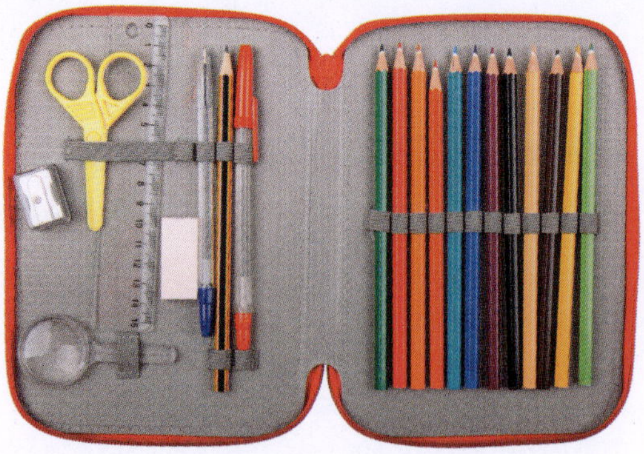

Activity 2.1b Doodle page

Things I love about me and my life...

Lesson 2 Cyberbullying

Activity 2.2a Top tips to deal with online bullying/trolls

1. However much you want to respond to their lies and cruel comments about you, don't. Replying will show them that they have upset you, which is what they are trying to do.
2. Report them to the moderator of the site on which the message was sent. The providers of platforms such as X and Facebook have a legal and moral duty to protect you. If the comment is hateful, report it to the police and remember always to ask an adult to help and support you.
3. Block the trolls from contacting you.
4. When you receive any message that is hurtful, your first reaction may be to delete it. Whatever you do, don't keep on reading it, or you're likely to get more and more upset. But don't delete it either. Save it or screenshot it. You may need it as evidence of how the troll is trying to get at you.
5. Don't suffer in silence. Tell an adult you can trust.
6. Don't try to sort it out alone. Sharing what's happening will help you to work out a strategy for dealing with it.
7. Never forward hurtful or embarrassing messages or photos of someone else. Delete them or report them to an adult you trust.
8. Inform the school, even if it's taking place outside school. They may be able to help.
9. Contact the police and show them the copies of the messages that you have kept.
10. Encourage anyone else you know who has been targeted to speak out and report it.

Which tips do you think are the most important and why? ______________________

Can you reduce each tip to two words (e.g. number 1. don't respond, 2. report them).

____

____

____

____

____

____

____

Lesson 2 Cyberbullying

Activity 2.2b Building up your confidence

If you or a friend have been bullied online, follow the guidance below to set about rebuilding your confidence.

1. **Share how you feel with someone you can trust to listen to you** – an adult such as a teacher, parent, sibling, grandparent or friend.
2. **Remember it isn't your fault.** You may have begun to feel that you must have done something wrong and that you deserve to be bullied. But if hurtful messages about you are being posted online, you aren't to blame. It's the bully who is responsible.
3. **Don't respond.** The bullies want to get a reaction from you. It makes them feel powerful and gives them a chance to continue attacking you. Instead of responding, which will only make it worse, switch off your phone or tablet and do something active.
4. **Take a cyber break.** The easiest way to avoid being affected by what is being said about you on social media is to take a break from using social media and the internet for a while. What you don't see or hear being said about you cannot affect you. The more you can push the bullying to the back of your mind, the less it will affect you.
5. **Try something new.** If you find it difficult to stop checking what the bullies are saying about you, try doing something different to take your mind off the bullying. You could join a group playing a new game or be the first person to reply to a message. You could use the internet to research a topic that interests you.
6. **Take action against the bullying.** Don't allow bullying to make you feel worthless. Use the anger you feel to take action against the bully. Collect evidence by taking a screenshot of what they are doing. Then block them and report them.
7. **Put it in writing.** Either keep a diary in which you write about your feelings or write yourself notes in which you remind yourself that it's not your fault that you are being bullied, that you are not going to respond to what they post and express how you intend to use your anger positively against them. You can put what you write in a box so that you can read the notes at times when the bullying leaves you feeling low.

Which piece of advice do you think is the most useful and why?

____

What else might help someone who has been bullied online to regain their confidence?

____

____

____

Lesson 3 Finding balance

Activity 2.3a A normal week

Think back to the previous week and complete the timetable below with all the activities you did, e.g. meal times, school, relaxing, studying at home/homework, exercising, having fun, seeing friends, quiet time, sleeping, being with family.

Time	Monday	Tuesday	Wednesday	Thursday	Friday	Saturday	Sunday
morning							
lunchtime							
afternoon							
dinner time							
evening							

Lesson 3 Finding balance

Activity 2.3b Sorting and reflecting

Using the information about your daily activities, sort the timetable contents into different 'buckets' on the scales – you will see one side is labelled 'self-care' and the other is 'school/work'. You can either draw these things or write the words in a pile on top of each bucket.

Unit reflection

Now that you've completed this unit, consider what you have learned about choosing kindness, for yourself and others, and how this can positively impact us all.

You can show what you have learned by drawing or writing below.

Unit 9.3 Looking after our bodies

What do you know?

- What do you like to consume for food and drink?
- Is it good for you?

In this unit, you will:

- Learn the importance of what vitamins and minerals do.
- Understand the impacts of unhealthy eating.
- Learn about prescription drug use.

Lesson 1 Vitamins and minerals

Activity 3.1a Healthy food

Write down all of the healthy foods you can think of. Which one of these do you eat the most? And which one is your favourite?

Write down everything you know about vitamins and minerals. Show it to your parent/ guardian and discuss why they are necessary. Are there any foods rich in either that you have mentioned above?

Lesson 1 Vitamins and minerals

Activity 3.1b My notes on vitamins and minerals

With seven of your friends, pick a vitamin and mineral each (you can write each on tiny bits of paper and draw lots to make it more fun and random). Look up the mineral or vitamin on the internet, and make notes on how it helps the body and the foods that are rich in them. Add any other information about it that you wish to add. Share the information with your friends and family.

Lesson 2 Unhealthy eating

Activity 3.2a Junk food

You have one minute to write down all of the junk food that you can think of.

Lesson 2 Unhealthy eating

Activity 3.2b Comic strip

It's time to create a comic about healthy eating!

Draw, with dialogues, a comic strip below that features a character named Esther Eatwell, who tries to encourage another character, Sam Snackalot, why he should stop snacking so much and stick to a healthy diet.

Lesson 3 Prescription drugs

Activity 3.3a What do you know about prescription medication?

Create a mind map around this image of everything you can think of about medicine, prescriptions and medications.

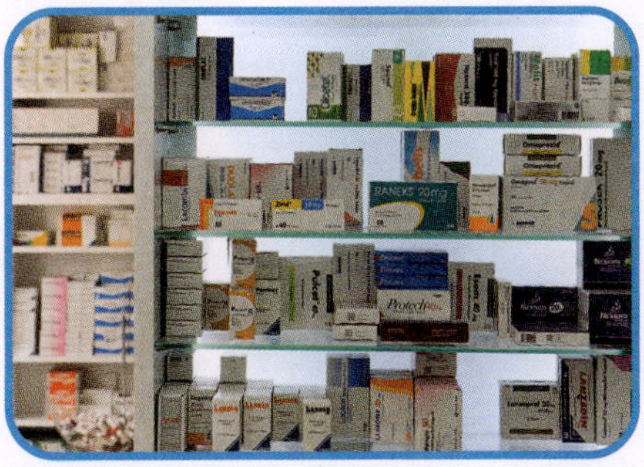

Lesson 3 Prescription drugs

Activity 3.3b Risky thoughts

Fill in the thought bubbles with a range of thoughts that someone might have when trying to make decisions on the risky situation of using medication that is not prescribed for them. Afterwards, discuss this with your guardian and other adults in your family, and if there's any prescribed medication that they're taking.

Unit reflection

Write a poem or short story about someone who accepts help from a friend with an issue such as unhealthy eating or prescription drug misuse.

Unit 9.4 Understanding one another

What do you know?

- About personal boundaries?
- About discrimination?
- What is going on in the image?

In this unit, you will:

- Learn about setting and respecting boundaries.
- Learn how to challenge discrimination and stereotypes.

Lesson 1 Our boundaries

Activity 4.1a Everyone is different!

Time for an activity on boundaries. With a trusted adult, practise how close is too close to someone. One of you will stand in a corner, while the other will take steps towards them. The person in the corner has to decide at what point is the other person too close for comfort. Afterwards, discuss this activity with your parent/guardian.

To complete at the beginning of the lesson

My measurement for how close was comfortable with my partner was ____________________

____

I knew it was my boundary because I felt ____________________________________

____

To complete later

What would make your boundaries feel respected? Consider this in different contexts (e.g. family, friends, at school or work, etc.).

____

____

____

____

____

____

How could you communicate your boundaries to these different groups of people in a positive manner?

____

____

____

____

____

____

____

____

____

____

Lesson 1 Our boundaries

Activity 4.1b Azim's story

Azim was seventeen. He had been a really well-behaved and kind boy all his life. He didn't like to upset anyone, so he got into the habit of keeping quiet and saying yes, even when he actually really wanted to say no.

He put up with his big brother bullying him and tried to fit in and be the person his parents wanted him to be, but he felt different about things from them.

They liked designer labels, fast cars and restaurants – he liked nature and simple things.

As he got older, he became more and more uncomfortable in their fast-paced world. He liked going for walks in nature and being quiet, but he went along with what they liked to keep them happy.

On his eighteenth birthday his family insisted on planning a huge party. However, he really didn't want one – he wanted to go hiking with his friends. But his family didn't ask him what he wanted, as usual, so he didn't say anything.

One day his best friend told him it was about time he thought about his needs and wants and stopped "people pleasing". He said Azim needed to get more honest with his family, say no to the party and tell them what he really wanted to do. He couldn't sleep worrying about it. Why couldn't he just say no?

What do you think of Azim's problem?

Is his friend right or wrong? Why?

Why do you think Azim is so worried? Discuss with your guardian and family what it means to be a 'people pleaser', and if that is always a good trait to have.

Lesson 2 Others' boundaries

Activity 4.2a Building boundaries

What do you remember about building your boundaries from the last lesson? Use the image as the middle of your mind map and write everything you learned, have been thinking about, have questions about or maybe have put in place since the last lesson.

Lesson 2 Others' boundaries

Activity 4.2b Reflecting on boundaries

> "Boundaries are the distance at which I can love you and me simultaneously."
>
> Prentis Hemphill

What does this quote mean to you personally? Try to explain in as much detail as you can. (There is no right or wrong answer.)

Now write a quote of your own. It doesn't have to be amazingly poetic or inspirational; it can simply be a reminder to yourself about something. You can illustrate this if you wish.

Lesson 3 Discrimination

Activity 4.3a What do you know?

Write or draw everything you know about discrimination.

Lesson 3 Discrimination

Activity 4.3b Matching activity

Discrimination is a term used to describe 'the practice of treating one person or group of people less fairly or less well than other people or groups'. *[Collins Dictionary]* Write the answers to questions 2 and 3 in your notebook.

1. Below are some examples of discrimination, including their meanings (from Collins Dictionary), along with some terms associated with them. However, the terms and their meanings are jumbled up. Your task is to connect the term to the correct meaning by drawing a line between the two boxes.

Term	Meaning
1. Prejudice	**a.** The belief that people of some races are inferior to others, and the behaviour which is the result of this belief. [It] also refers to the aspects of a society which prevent people of some racial groups from having the same privileges and opportunities as people from other races.
2. Stereotype	**b.** The belief that older people are of less value than younger people.
3. Racism	**c.** Discrimination against disabled people.
4. Ageism	**d.** An unreasonable dislike of a particular group of people or things, or a preference for one group of people or things over another.
5. Ableism	**e.** A fixed general image or set of characteristics that a lot of people believe represent a particular type of person or thing.

2. Sadly, these are just a few examples of the many different types of discrimination against certain characteristics. Can you think of any other examples you might have heard about?

3. Can you explain why you think stereotypical thinking can make discrimination worse? Explain your answer and if you are not sure just write down your thoughts and discuss it with the adults in your family.

Unit reflection

Can you write a poem about kindness? It doesn't have to rhyme – it's just your thoughts and feelings on being kind to ourselves and others. You can use anything you learned about in this unit and mix it with your own ideas however you wish. Add illustrations or decorate this page in any way you want once your poem is complete.

Unit 9.5 Us and the wider world

What do you know?

- How many people do you think live in
  - your neighbourhood?
  - your country?
  - the world?

  Have a guess and check your answers at the end of the unit!

In this unit, you will:

- Learn how to be a true ally.
- Understand the importance of communities and your place in them.
- Learn about the laws that affect you.

Lesson 1 Becoming a better ally

Activity 5.1a What is an ally?

1. What's happening here?

2. What is an ally? Look up its definition in the dictionary and discuss with your parent/guardian the meaning of the term here.

Lesson 1 Becoming a better ally

Activity 5.1b Learning how to be an ally

To be a true ally, you need to ask questions and listen to people you don't know that well to understand them better so that you can be of help. Think of a group of people in your society who you do not know much about – this could be locally or nationally. You are going to research these people to really understand them, and then consider how you could ally themselves with them, e.g. someone with a different religion, culture, identity. Write your notes below.

Lesson 2 Our communities

Activity 5.2a My communities

Write your name in the middle of this sun. Then add the different communities you belong to at the end of the sun rays. Also discuss with your parent/guardian and add what roles and actions you are expected to perform as a member of various communities.

Lesson 2 Our communities

Activity 5.2b Photo opportunity!

Click photos of your family members and friends (with their permission) as they are carrying out tasks of being a member of their respective communities. Ask them about it and think if there are any similar tasks that you are encouraged or asked to do. You can add photos here with annotations written beside them to describe what is happening in the picture and what you think of being part of this community/what it gives you.

Lesson 3 Us and the law

Activity 5.3a Laws!

What do you know? Write everything you know about laws and the legal system and discuss it with an adult in your family.

Lesson 3 Us and the law

Activity 5.3b At what age does the law apply?

- Look at the table. Use the internet to help you fill in at what age you think you are able to do each of the activities. Just fill in this first column for now. Then check your answers with your parent/guardian.

Law	What age?	Fair or unfair?	Why do you think this?
Allowed to leave school			
Have a bank account in your name			
Drive a car			
Start going to school full-time			
Get married with a parent's consent			
Be sent to prison			
Sign a legal contract			
Be convicted of a criminal offence if it can be proved you knew you were doing something wrong			
Have your own passport			

- Now, write down whether you think each of these age limits is fair or unfair, with any reasons for your views in the last column.
- Finally, discuss the age limits with your parent/guardian, giving reasons for your views.

Unit reflection

At the beginning of this unit you guessed how many people you think live in

- your neighbourhood
- your country
- the world.

Find out how close you were by using the internet to find the correct figures. Write them below.

What positive changes can you make in your life to give more to the world? Give three simple pledges below – these can be related to being an ally or getting more involved in your community, for example.

1.

2.

3.

Unit 9.6 Being safety conscious

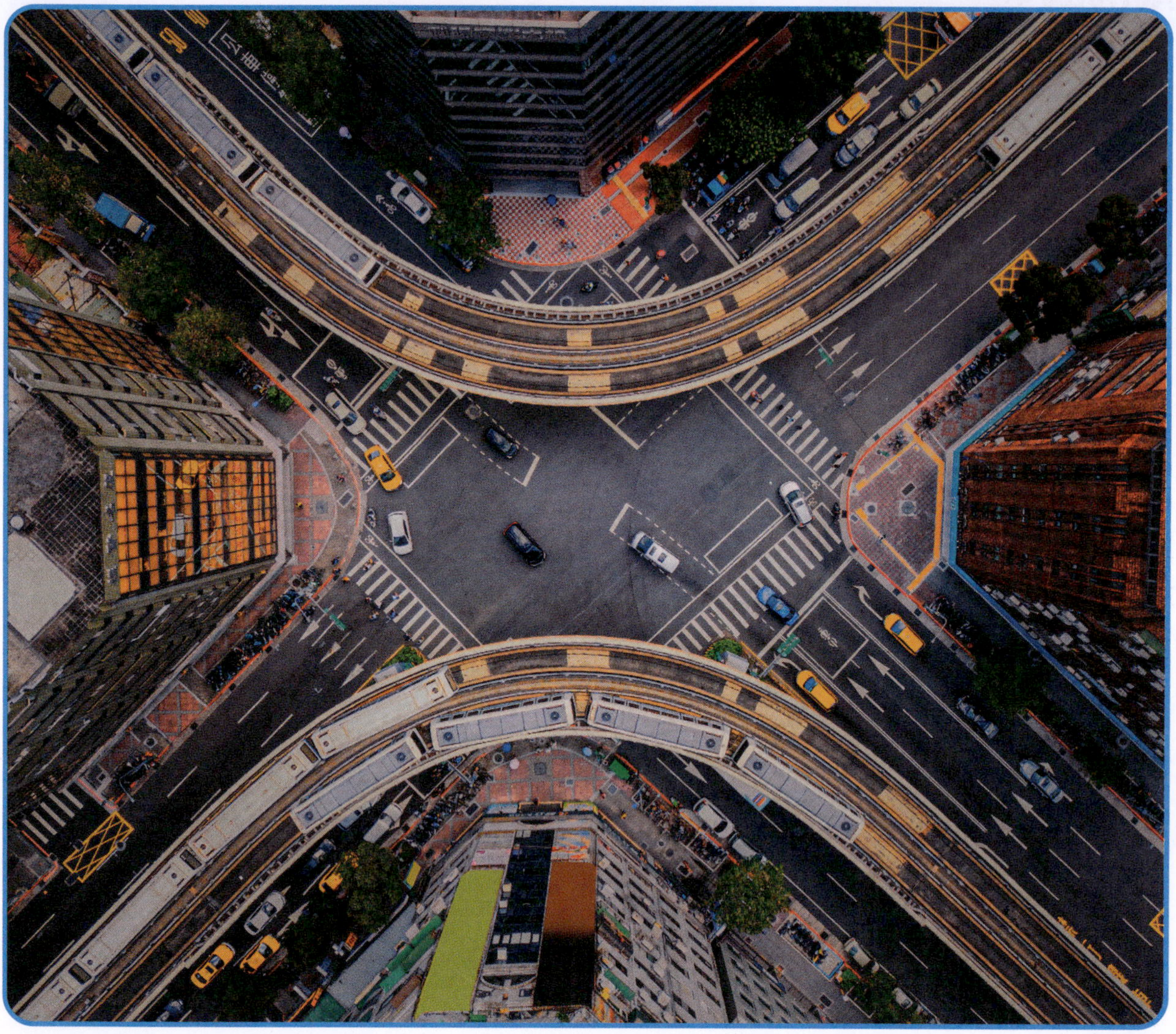

What do you know?

- Spot the potential dangers in this picture.
- Think about the places and what could happen there too.

In this unit, you will:

- Learn about how to drive and be a passenger safely.
- Consider what risky behaviour is and why teenagers are particularly prone.
- Learn what to do if a violent situation looks like it is escalating.

Lesson 1 Keeping safe on the roads

Activity 6.1a Modes of transport

Thinking about all the different modes of transport, write everything you can think of about keeping safe when in or on them.

Lesson 1 Keeping safe on the roads

Activity 6.1b Advice from the UK government for new drivers

Many of the worst collisions happen at night. Between midnight and 6 a.m. is a time of high risk for new drivers. Avoid driving then unless it's really necessary.

If you are driving with passengers, you are responsible for their safety. Don't let them distract you or encourage you to take risks. Tell your passengers that you need to concentrate if you are to get to your destination safely.

Never show off or try to compete with other drivers, particularly if they are driving badly...

Over-the-counter medicines can affect your ability to drive safely – read the label to see if they may affect your driving.

Make sure everyone in the car is wearing a seat belt throughout the journey.

Keep your speed down – many serious collisions happen because the driver loses control, particularly on bends...

Most new drivers have no experience of driving high-powered or sporty cars. Unless you have learned to drive in such a vehicle you need to get plenty of experience driving on your own before driving a more powerful car.

Driving while uninsured is an offence. See 'Motor vehicle documentation and learner driver requirements' for information on types of insurance cover...

[From GOV.UK]

Is there anything you can add to this or that you would change for your country?

Lesson 2 Risky behaviour

Activity 6.2a What's happening?

1. What's happening here?

2. What do you think about this?

3. If this person likes climbing, how could he do this in a safe way and place? Write or draw your ideas below.

Lesson 2 Risky behaviour

Activity 6.2b The adolescent brain

Write down how the teenage brain works in different areas. (You can also add comparisons with a fully developed adult brain if you wish.)

1. ______________________________

2. ______________________________

3. ______________________________

4. ______________________________

5. ______________________________

What does this tell you about the teenage brain? ______________________________

Why does this show that teenagers need to think extra carefully before doing any risky behaviours? ______________________________

Lesson 3 Staying safe on the streets

Activity 6.3a Potential trigger points

Where might situations escalate to aggressive or violent behaviour? Look at the map below and circle all the areas that you think could be a potential trigger spot for violence. Then write why you think this.

Lesson 3 Staying safe on the streets

Activity 6.3b De-escalating aggression.

When people get angry or feel threatened, their emotions can escalate very quickly. 'Escalation' is what is happening inside these people's bodies as their emotions build - this is called a 'fight response'. A number of different chemicals race through a person at such a time, and also those who are encouraging them. They will almost certainly be unable to think about the consequences of their actions, and will not listen to 'reason' either. This is why, after violent events, people end up saying things like 'I don't know what came over me', or 'I can't believe I did that.'

Sit with your parent/guardian and discuss how one can stay away from such events happening, and also help in de-escalating the situation. Make your notes below.

Lesson 3 Staying safe on the streets

Activity 6.3b De-escalating aggression

Imagine two groups of friends. Then imagine that two people, one from each group, have got into an argument – this could be face to face or online. The situation is escalating. Remembering what you have learned, consider what you could do to de-escalate this aggressive behaviour. Consider before the event/confrontation, the build-up as emotions get stronger, and during the event. Then create a comic strip to show what you would do. You can choose to focus on a face-to-face situation, a situation on social media, or a mixture of the two.

Unit reflection

Look at the images. What did you learn in these lessons?

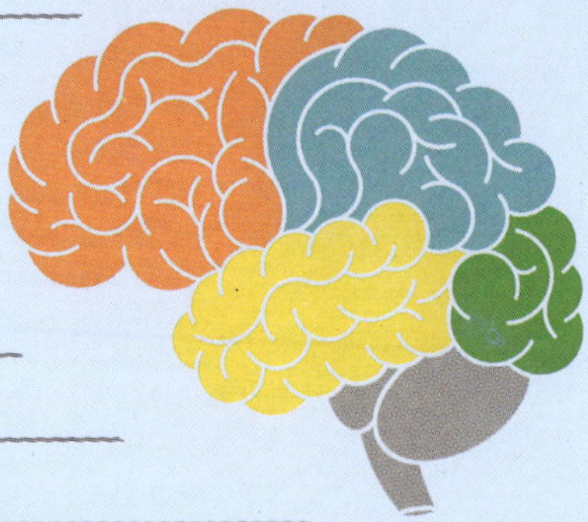

Is there anything you don't understand or need to know more about?

Unit 9.7 Facing challanges

What do you know?

- About facing challenges?
- What do you think are negative and positive changes in life?

In this unit, you will:

- Learn how to manage positive and negative changes.
- Understand how mistakes and imperfections are better for us than perfection.
- Find strategies for problem-solving and to build resilience.

Lesson 1 Getting ready for change

Activity 7.1a Becoming an adult

What are you looking forward to about being an adult? Write or draw them all here.

Lesson 1 Getting ready for change

Activity 7.1b Skills for independence

How did you do?

Being an adult has its positives and negatives, but one of the things that defines adulthood is independence. This independence comes with not just a lot of fun, but a lot of responsibilities too. As an adult, you have to learn to do a lot of things by yourself. With your parent/guardian, learn some of the basic household chores that you will be doing as an adult. Ask them to teach you and let you make your own bed, your laundry, as well as learning how to make something basic like a salad or scrambled eggs. Good luck!

1. How were your bed-making skills? What did you learn? Have you improved, and if so, how?

____

____

____

____

____

____

____

2. How were your salad-making skills? What did you learn? Have you improved, and if so, how?

____

____

____

____

____

3. How were your laundry-sorting skills? What did you learn? Have you improved, and if so, how?

____

____

____

____

____

Lesson 2 Imperfection vs perfection

Activity 7.2a Perfectionism

Perfectionism means quite simply wanting things to be the best they can – to be perfect.

Below are some philosophical questions for you to consider on this subject. This worksheet isn't about being 'right'. It has been developed for you to think deeply about these questions, so allow your ideas and thoughts to flow freely. Feel free to discuss these with your friends or siblings as well.

Statement	Agree or disagree?	Why do you think this?
Is perfection equal to success?		
Is perfection equal to being the best?		
Is perfection being true to yourself?		
Does perfectionism lead to a happier life?		
Does perfectionism divide us?		

Further comments or questions: ______________________________

____

____

____

____

____

____

____

Lesson 2 Imperfection vs perfection

Activity 7.2b Embracing mistakes

1. Explore the idea of seeing mistakes as opportunities to grow and to learn as opposed to being perfect. What might this look like in day-to-day life? How would it feel? Write your thoughts on this below and discuss them with your parent/guardian.

2. Now consider how it would feel to allow yourself to be 'good enough' rather than perfect. Write your thoughts on this below.

Lesson 3 Solving problems, building resilience

Activity 7.3a Overcoming problems

Think of a time when you were stuck with something or a problem that was particularly difficult that you managed to overcome. What difficult problem have you overcome?

How did you overcome it?

How long did you take to overcome this problem?

What did you learn from this?

Lesson 3 Solving problems, building resilience

Activity 7.3a Overcoming Problems

There are two main ways to solve a problem that lets it be broken down into simpler steps, which makes it easier to solve and does not overwhelm us.

Lesson 3 Solving problems, building resilience

Activity 7.3b Resilience

"What strategies can I employ to make me more resilient so that I will deal better with a problem?" Read through the strategies below and make notes beneath each one.

1. What problem do I have with my learning or anything else at present?

   ____

   ____

2. Time management – set a clear time and place where you will deal with the problem.

   ____

   ____

3. Dealing with anxiety – strategies could include breathing, relaxation, meditation, yoga or talking the problem out with a friend, parent/guardian, tutor or counsellor. What would work for you?

   ____

   ____

4. Breaking the problem down – breaking the problem into a series of small easy steps can make it feel much more manageable. How could this work for your problem?

   ____

   ____

5. Just start it – sometimes a good way to start dealing with a problem is to dive right in to make some progress, rather than putting it off. Remember, you can take your time to get it right. When can you get started? ______________________________

   ____

6. Worry time – if a problem is hanging over you, allocate yourself a maximum of 20 minutes, and only 20 minutes, a day to worry about it. For the rest of the day, enjoy yourself and be present in the moment. When could you allocate this worry time?

   ____

   ____

Other (add your own ideas – you will know what works well for you): ______________________________

____

____

Unit reflection

Dear diary,

In this unit I learned about how to face challenges. I learned

Unit 9.8 Taking action

What do you want to shout about?

In this unit, you will:

- Learn about the connection between sustainability and wellbeing.
- Make some big changes at your school.
- Raise your voice for your local community.

Lesson 1 Sustainability and wellbeing

Activity 8.1a Research notes

You might already have learned in school about sustainable development. But how is sustainable development connected to wellbeing? Go online to the UN website, and go through in detail the Sustainable Development Goals that the UN has. After you've done your research, write notes on the different goals, and which UN Sustainable Development Goal resonates the most with you and why.

Lesson 1 Sustainability and wellbeing

Activity 8.1b Connections

Where do you see the most obvious connections between sustainability and wellbeing? Write your ideas in the tree.

Lesson 2 Sustainable travel campaign

Activity 8.2 Notes

Now that you have learned about sustainability and its importance to our wellbeing, it's time to take action and start your own sustainable travel campaign. Remember, you will need the help of a lot of people for this, so try to rope in as many friends, family members, classmates and teachers into it.

To decrease the pollution and environmental impact of cars, you will aim to get as many people as you can to walk, cycle, or use public transport in your local neighbourhood.

- Find evidence to show the environmental impact car driving has.
- Find evidence of why the school making this change is important in order to encourage others to take part.
- Consider how best to do a survey to see what students' mode of transport is at present.
- Record all this information and bring it together in an action plan to pitch to the head of school, senior leadership team and governors.

Lesson 2 Sustainable travel campaign

Activity 8.2 Notes continued

Lesson 3 My community, my views

Activity 8.3a The UN Rights of the Child

What do I remember about the UN Rights of the Child? Write what you can remember, using the text below as the centre of your mind map.

UN Rights of the Child

Lesson 3 My community, my views

Activity 8.3b Preparing my speech

Choose a topic affecting children's rights and express your views by writing a speech. What do you want to say to support, challenge or change?

Use this page to write down ideas and plan your speech.

Unit reflection

How can I take action?

Tell the world what action for others you are going to take, reflecting on all the things you have learned in this lesson.

TAKE ACTION

Acknowledgements

The Publishers wish to thank the following for permission to reproduce image and copyright material. Every effort has been made to trace copyright holders and to obtain their permission for the use of copyright materials. The publishers will gladly receive any information enabling them to rectify any error or omission at the first opportunity.

7.2.1. An extract and illustration from "The girl who fell from the sky" by Juliane Koepeke, published in Survivors by David Long, illustrated by Kerry Hyndman, Faber & Faber Limited, 2017, text copyright © David Long, 2016, illustrations copyright © Kerry Hyndman, 2016. Reproduced with permission of the publisher; **7.5.2**. An extract about Peer Pressure, Childline, https://www.childline.org.uk/info-advice/friends-relationships-sex/friends/peer-pressure/. Reproduced with permission; **7.6.1**. An extract adapted from "I am setting up a new social media account" Internet Matters, https:// www. internetmatters.org/connecting-safely-online/advice-for-young-people/do-the-basics-on-social-media/i-am-setting-up-anew- social-account/. Reproduced with permission; **7.8.1**. An extract from "Why buy ethically?" Ethical Consumer website http://www.ethicalconsumer.org/shoppingethically/whybuyethical.aspx. Reproduced with permission; **7.8.2**. An extract from "Living Planet Report 2022" WWF, https://livingplanet.panda.org. Reproduced with permission; **7.8.3**. An extract from "Universal Declaration of Human Rights" Amnesty International, https://www.amnesty.org/en/what-we-do/universaldeclaration-of-human-rights/. Reproduced by permission of Amnesty International; and **7.8.3**. Extracts and images from "The Convention of the Rights of the Child: Children's Version" Unicef, https://www.unicef.org/child-rights-convention/convention-text-childrens-version. Paraphrased from articles on pp.49–50 from "Summary of The United Nations Convention on the Rights of the Child", https://downloads.unicef.org.uk/wp-content/uploads/2019/10/UNCRC_summary-1_1.pdf. Reproduced by permission of Unicef UK. **9.1.3**. Diagram of the grief cycle, adapted from On Grief and Grieving by Elizabeth Kübler-Ross and David Kessler, 2014, copyright © 2005 by Elisabeth Kübler-Ross Family Limited Partnership and David Kessler, Inc. Reproduced with the permission of Scribner, a division of Simon & Schuster, Inc. All rights reserved; **9.2.1**. Extract from "Confi dence and self-esteem for 11-18 year olds" MIND, https:// www.mind.org.uk/for-young-people/ feelings-and-experiences/confi dence-and-self-esteem/. Reproduced with permission; **9.4.2**. A quotation by Prentis Hemphill, Founder of The Embodiment Institute, https://prentishemphill.com/; 9.4.2. Defi nitions of 'Discrimination,' 'Prejudice,' 'Racism,' 'Ageism' and 'Ableism' from Collins Dictionary. Reproduced by permission of the HarperCollins Publishers Ltd; **9.6.1**. An extract from The Highway Code, Annex 8. Safety code for new drivers, https://www.gov.uk/guidance/thehighway-code/annex-8-safety-code-for-new-drivers, © Crown Copyright. All content is available under the Open Government Licence v3.0; and **9.8.3**. Images from "The Convention of the Rights of the Child: Children's Version" Unicef, https://www. unicef.org/child-rights-convention/convention-text-childrens-version. Paraphrased from articles on pp.49–50 from "Summary of The United Nations Convention on the Rights of the Child", https://downloads.unicef.org.uk/wp-content/uploads/2019/10/UNCRC_summary-1_1.pdf. Reproduced by permission of Unicef UK. **7.1.1** Rawpixel.com/ Shutterstock, Crocolot/ Shutterstock, WS **7.1.1** Christoph Burgstedt/ Shutterstock, **7.1.2** ileezhun/ Shutterstock, **7.1.3** newelle/Shutterstock, VikiVector/Shutterstock, Julia Bessonova/ Shutterstock, **7.2.1** Martin73/ Shutterstock, Uuganbayar/ Shutterstock, **7.2.2** Crystal Eye Studio/ Shutterstock, **7.3.1** imtmphoto/ Shutterstock, **7.5.1** kuroksta/ Shutterstock, Tang Yan Song/Shutterstock, bht2000/ Shutterstock, **7.5.3** tomertu/ Shutterstock, ishivaaym/ Shutterstock, **7.6.1** 19srb81/ Shutterstock, Rawpixel.com/ Shutterstock, **7.6.2** rickyd/ Shutterstock, PR Image Factory/ Shutterstock, Herwin Bahar/ Shutterstock (editorial use only), De Visu/ Shutterstock, Ground Picture/ Shutterstock, rjankovsky/ Shutterstock, Mamunur Rashid/ Shutterstock, Soloviova Liudmyla/ Shutterstock, 7.6.3 Vitalii Vodolazskyi/ Shutterstock, HowLettery/ Shutterstock, 7.7.1 Thinglass/ Shutterstock, 7.7.2 PradeepGaurs/ Shutterstock, 7.7.3 JennyJukker/ Shutterstock, BrightRainbow/ Shutterstock, 7.8.1 iQoncept/ Shutterstock, Taras Grebinets/ Shutterstock, ingehogenbijl/ Shutterstock, Kaspars Grinvalds/ Shutterstock, 7.8.2 WB Captain Wang/ Shutterstock, MMD Creative/ Shutterstock, 8.1.1 ChristianChan/ Shutterstock, MisterStock/ Shutterstock, 8.1.2 kuroksta/ Shutterstock, 8.2.1 Sofi aworld/ Shutterstock, WS 8.2.1 tannikart/ Shutterstock, 8.2.2 Mr-Y/ Shutterstock, Simbert Brause/ Shutterstock, MichaelJayBerlin/ Shutterstock, WS 8.2.2 Simbert Brause/ Shutterstock, 8.2.3 Ekaterina_Minaeva/ Shutterstock, YasnaTen/ Shutterstock, 8.3.1 Pop Paul-Catalin/ Shutterstock, 8.3.2 AV-Art/ Shutterstock, 8.3.3 MoonRock/ Shutterstock, Claudio Divizia/ Shutterstock, 8.4.1 PiconsMe/ Shutterstock, The Studio/ Shutterstock, 8.4.2 Alphavector/ Shutterstock, 8.4.3 BNP Design Studio/ Shutterstock, Nor Sham Soyod/ Shutterstock, 8.5.1 solarseven/ Shutterstock, Roman Samborskyi/ Shutterstock, 8.5.2 PhotoBankIndia/ Shutterstock, Maharani afi fah/ Shutterstock, 8.5.3 pathdoc/ Shutterstock, 8.6.1 ESB Professional/ Shutterstock, Jacob Lund/ Shutterstock, tilialucida/ Shutterstock, 8.6.3 Prostock-studio/ Shutterstock, Boonker/ Shutterstock, patpitchaya/ Shutterstock, 8.7.1 metamorworks/ Shutterstock, 8.7.2 Dragon Images/ Shutterstock, 8.7.3 yayhastudio/ Shutterstock, Rawpixel.com/ Shutterstock, 8.8.1 Delpixel/ Shutterstock, Bored Photography/ Shutterstock, Carkhe/ Shutterstock, WS 8.8.1 Carkhe/ Shutterstock, 8.8.2 SB Kev Gregory/ Shutterstock, Stefan Milivojevic/

Shutterstock, reddees, Martin Prochazkacz/ Shutterstock, eamesBot/ Shutterstock, 8.8.3 PremiumArt/Shutterstock, 9.1.1 Alex_Po/ Shutterstock, Matusciac Alexandru/ Shutterstock, 9.2.1 Mitoria/ Shutterstock, conzorb/ Shutterstock,9.2.3 smx12/ Shutterstock, 9.3.1 Thiti Sukapan/ Shutterstock, 9.3.2 OlgaChernyak/ Shutterstock, 9.3.3 Lestertair/ Shutterstock, Lidiia Koval/ Shutterstock, WS 9.3.3 Lidiia Koval/ Shutterstock, 9.4.1 SB Vitalii Vodolazskyi/ Shutterstock, Ariya J/ Shutterstock, 9.4.2 Nadia Snopek/ Shutterstock, 9.4.3 anna.spoka/ Shutterstock, 9.5.1 oneinchpunch/ Shutterstock, Vitalii Vodolazskyi/ Shutterstock, melitas/ Shutterstock, WS 9.5.1 Vitezslav Valka/ Shutterstock, 9.5.2 Noushad Thekkayil/ Shutterstock, BadaL_ studio/ Shutterstock, 9.5.3 Net Vector/ Shutterstock, 9.6.1 Tavarius/ Shutterstock, PremiumStock/ Shutterstock, WS 9.6.1 PremiumStock/ Shutterstock, lazyllama/ Shutterstock, 9.6.2 bsd studio/ Shutterstock, shopplaywood/ Shutterstock, 9.6.3 WB Shayne T Wright/ Shutterstock, 9.7.1 Miller Inna/ Shutterstock, fi zkes/ Shutterstock, Dusan Petkovic/ Shutterstock, WS 9.7.1 (t) Dusan Petkovic/ Shutterstock, WS 9.7.1

The Wellbeing for Kids Series